Review by Neepa DeVries, Bible teacher

Marnie's story is, in some ways, all our stories. It is, above all, a story of the hope that God holds out to us all. No matter how badly we may have lost our way, no matter how blind we have been to God's goodness and mercy, God's voice and God's heart powerfully draws us to Him for redemption and the hope of restoration. Marnie's life is a demonstration of what God can do in a vessel yielded to Him in obedience and love. One can almost see the change in Marnie from the early stages of the book where she is striving to find God to the place where she begins to find increasing joy in walking with Jesus. In the pages of this book, you will find renewed hope, joy and encouragement to keep walking with Jesus.

NONE CAN Compare

A NOVEL

BY MARSHA BLACKFORD

XULON PRESS ELITE

Xulon Press Elite
2301 Lucien Way #415
Maitland, FL 32751
407.339.4217
www.xulonpress.com

Paperback ISBN-13: 978-1-66283-583-4
Ebook ISBN-13: 978-1-66283-584-1

Table of Contents

About the Author

MARSHA BLACKFORD FIRST ENCOUN-tered Jesus while working in an abortion clinic. Much like the stiff-necked Hebrew people in the wilderness, she had a direct word from God. But she at first turned to idols. She knew that abortion was murder and quit. She knew that Jesus loved her and forgave her. But she stubbornly ignored Him for 30 years. That crazy decision got her involved with the Hare Krishna movement. After 25 years in that cult, 13 of which she ran the society's newspaper, the author met a man of God. He led her into Christ's Kingdom once and for all, and they married happily. She is now widowed and volunteers at a Christian crisis pregnancy center, and she prays for you.

The author invites readers to also check out her first Christian novel, "Amanda's Song."

Acknowledgments

I WANT TO THANK SHARON SHIELDS, MY dear friend, for patiently listening and critiquing this story as I read page after page to her discerning heart. Her concrete mind helped craft explanations of religious practices that are foreign to most readers. Please keep in mind that people who follow false religions sincerely believe they are serving God. The absolute unchanging Truth, Jesus Christ, yearns to free them. That may go for some lukewarm Christians, as well—just saying.

I also considerably owe to my pastors, Edwin and Angela Anderson, whose ministrations from the pulpit have strengthened my trust in God's Word. Their uncompromising faith teaching and personal integrity have inspired generations. I am grateful to be planted in their midst at Impact Family Church.

Finally, I dedicate this work to my Savior and God, King Jesus. He told me to write it. He gave me the words and the audacity to believe that something good could come of so much bad. I don't care how many devils it stirs up. I know Who is for me. Thank you, dear Lord. You are my life, and I commit this story into Your prospering. I ask for and expect angel assistance to save, heal, deliver, and bless many.

None Can Compare
A Novel
By Marsha Blackford

Prologue

Psalm 135:15–18 (ESV)

"The idols of the nations are silver and gold, the work of human hands. They have mouths, but do not speak; they have eyes, but do not see; they have ears, but do not hear, nor is there any breath in their mouths. Those who make them become like them, so do all who trust in them."

"WHAT'S HE DOING? SHEILA ASKED ME.

"The priest is worshipping Krishna," I answered, as the saffron-robed man swished a peacock feather fan on the altar.

"The little one at the front looks like a rock," she observed. The small black deity having a painted face and crown rested on a little golden throne draped with a fresh flower garland.

"It's a very holy manifestation of God, found only in a sacred river in India by a sadhu, a holy man," I clarified.

Sheila observed the ritual, which involved offering a variety of substances to opulently dressed male and female deities about four feet tall and made out of burnished metal. Some of the items were handed down to the worshippers by the priest and then passed around. The women stood mostly at the back, so it was a while before a brass holder with a smoldering ghee wick came to us in the crowded temple.

"You pass your hand over it to receive the fire of the Lord, like this." I demonstrated and then extended the lamp to her. Sheila half-heartedly waved her hand over the smoke. I passed it to the teenage girl waiting next to me.

During the worship ceremony, the devotees sang a ritualistic song in Sanskrit to the beating of a long, handheld mridanga drum and small cymbals. They next sat down on the marble floor to listen to a scripture reading and lecture. I neatly arranged my sari about my crossed legs, carefully pulling the veil that covered my hair. Sheila squirmed uncomfortably on the hard floor. I got up to search for one of the cushions provided for revered holy men, called sannyasis, and for guests. There were many important devotees there because a revered guru was present. Nimai, a bare-chested celibate student, or brahmachari, grabbed the last mat, scowled at me, and plunked down on it, proudly sweeping his saffron dhoti over his legs and bare feet. I sighed and sat down again.

Afterward, we retrieved our shoes and queued up outside to get a plate of the Sunday feast.

"What's this?" Sheila asked. She looked at the fragrant cooked vegetable mixture spooned onto a paper plate as we moved through the line.

"That's subji," I said.

"It smells like curry," she replied, as rice and then chutney and puri, a fried flat bread, were generously added to our plates.

"It's all prasadam," I explained cheerfully. "This isn't ordinary food. It's been offered to the deities on the altar. By eating the remnants of preparations lovingly offered to Krishna, you get rid of karma."

"They feed it to the statues on the altar?" Sheila was incredulous.

"That's right." I smiled. "But don't call them statues. They're the authorized deity form of God, Krishna, and his girlfriend, Radharani.

Sheila digested the idea that God had a girlfriend. "And you think eating it gets rid of sin?"

"That's right," I led her over to a picnic table where some of my friends were. "Everything we do at the temple is designed to rid us of our karma so we can join Krishna in his Vaikuntha planet when we leave our bodies. We don't want to come back here, especially as some lesser being."

It was obvious to me that Sheila was not ready to swallow all that. But she dug into her plate of vegetarian food and grinned at me. "It's pretty good, even if it is the leftovers of a rock."

Chapter 1

Psalm 19:14 (NIV)

"May these words of my mouth and this meditation of my heart be pleasing in your sight, Lord, my Rock and my Redeemer."

STUART AND I ATTENDED THE MEETING on campus not knowing what to expect. A college-age man stood up in front and asked if we knew what meditation was. Stuart raised his hand. I didn't.

After a passionate acclamation of the physical and spiritual benefits of this practice, the leader, or one of his assistants, individually took each of the thirty or so of us novices aside to another room and secretly whispered a word in our ear. We were sternly instructed to *never* say it aloud or share it with anyone. My word sounded like "I'm."

There was no mention of a unique sovereign higher being. There was the implication that by this method, we could find the power within ourselves to master our lives and become our own God. By the time my boyfriend and I got in the car to head home, we were shed of our precious $200 per person. But we'd been initiated into the popular and mysterious path of transcendental meditation, or TM.

Stuart eagerly took to TM. He would sit cross-legged in our bedroom twice a day. Eyes closed, he quieted his breathing and occupied the floor for a good 30 minutes or more. Since I was the one working with a full schedule, I meditated whenever I could. I rarely could sit for the prescribed 20-minute minimum. Emptying my mind of everything but that secret word (did I tell you it sounded like "I'm"?) was impossible for me. I asked Stuart about this. He said that he had no problem with it. He seemed so sure of himself. His speech had gotten softer, his body language loftier, and he didn't make much eye contact with me. If he did, I felt he was looking right through me without really seeing me. Anyway, I had to believe him.

One day, as I labored to enter into the inner spiritual realm (thinking "I'm"), the thought popped up, *Why don't you think of Me?* I answered in my head, *Who is Me?* There was no answer, but the question lingered for the next three years. Anyway, I tried to convince myself that I was my own God, soon to be merged with the great abstract universe. But I wasn't supposed to think of myself or to think of anything at all. I was just to concentrate on that stupid sound. Frustratingly, I still had heart needs that I couldn't satisfy by myself. Stuart continued to distance himself from me emotionally. Nothing made sense. I descended into confusion and discouragement.

After a couple of months, I told Stuart about my failure as a TM practitioner. He signed us up for another session. The leader took me aside and asked me what the problem was. His attitude shamed me. I denied I had a problem and lied. I said my meditations were going great. After staring at me a moment (no doubt with his own wheels turning), he proclaimed that I was ready for my more advanced secret meditation word. It sounded something like "i-ing-nama." This one sold for $300. Since Stuart didn't have enough, it actually cost me more like $500.

I really wanted to see results. I was hoping for peace and happiness. What I got was ignored and irritated. I mean, Stuart was unconcerned and impersonal. He took off for California to visit some friend with very little notice. While he was gone, I exercised, lost a little weight, and bought new sheets. When he returned, he made not one comment about my improved looks. That first night, he stayed up so late, I went to bed without him. If he and I were getting closer to our inner whatever, godliness or core meaning, and merging more and more into the common cosmos, why were we drifting apart? The more we meditated, the lonelier I got.

So I called Sheila. Now, Sheila is my best friend, but we're very different. I'm the seeker. She's not. I always want something more. She doesn't. Sometimes, I'd get upset with her contentment. It didn't seem fair. I was trying so hard to expand my mind and achieve spiritual perfection. Sheila just did the same old stuff she always did and was infuriatingly mellow.

She responded with her typically inane kind of proposal when I told her about my misery and Stuart's detachment. "You wanta come to church with me?" she asked.

Now, at this point, church was the last thing I wanted. I had already rejected Christianity as too simplistic and authoritarian. But I was so out of sorts at the time, I answered to my surprise that I'd go.

She picked me up Sunday morning. That was a big mistake. I was trapped into not only attending the entire service, but going out to lunch with her family afterwards. Her mother, who had never approved of me, scowled at my apparent lack of agreement with the preacher's sermon about Jesus Christ as the only way to God. Sheila, being the kind person she is, picked up on my discomfort and took me home, eventually. When I let myself into the empty apartment, my discontent turned to despair. Stuart's stuff was all gone. He took advantage of my absence to exit without even saying goodbye.

So I kicked TM to the curb and turned to feminism as my new path to truth and happiness. Oh, and I bought a baggie of pot, which I consumed rather quickly.

"This is our Bible," my new mentor, Sally, said while she handed me a booklet titled, "Our Bodies Our Selves." Back on the college campus, I'd attended a workshop on women's studies. I met her there. Sally was a heavy smoker and wore baggy men's trousers and an oversized T-shirt with no bra. "When you get done with that, you need to read these." She loaded me down with several more paperbacks, including *Feminine Mystique* and *Sexual Politics*. I thanked her, declined her invitation for a date, and went back to the apartment to get busy studying this exciting new way to truth and happiness in woman worship.

Chapter 2

Romans 13:13 (NIV)

"Let us behave decently, as in the daytime, not in carousing and drunkenness, not in sexual immorality and debauchery, not in dissension and jealousy."

THE FEMINIST PHILOSOPHY SEEMED steeped in bodily identification, with scant reference to spiritual things, except somewhat in a sexual context. I learned that feminists have good intentions toward women but not so much toward all people, meaning men. Christianity, and religion in general, got bashed as being macho and therefore anti-woman. However, there was a religion attached to feminism that became apparent. It was the worship of self. This was a little familiar to me because of my experience with TM. So I thought it was right. After all, what was the value of creation to me if I were not my own creator? If there was any question to the logic of that, I ignored it.

Since I now accepted that my body was myself, I had complete sovereignty over it. I ate whatever I wanted and gained 20 pounds. I drank wine and smoked pot with my new women friends. We partied, and some of them explored sexual pleasure with one another. I was still heterosexual, and I enjoyed flaunting it before the lesbians. Hey, it was *my* choice, and I didn't care what they thought about it. They teased me but said they didn't mind too much, as long as

I didn't *serve* a man (read "submit"). True to feminist form, I used men for my pleasure, not caring about how many guys I had sex with. Until I got an infection. Whoops.

Walking into the Feminist Health Center in my southern town was fresh air for me. Here were people who really cared about me. They quickly addressed my little medical problem and renewed my birth control. I took their self-help class and learned a lot about my body. I started volunteering there. Then, I got hired as a counselor and quit my other job. I was in bliss, doing what I wanted, with people I liked, *and* getting paid for it.

A dynamic lesbian couple started a credit union in the upstairs of the house that served as our clinic. Their goal was to help women who had been divorced or were underemployed to establish credit. They liberally gave loans so women could buy cars and meet other needs. The credit union grew rapidly. Their loyal customers paid off loans with interest. It became a growing concern, which eventually imploded. The directors were making a lot of money. Other women became envious. So much for sisterhood.

In the meanwhile, I was assisting our clients with wellness examinations. But there was another service that we offered, and it quickly became lucrative. Before long, we were primarily abortion providers. This brought some heat. Since the clinic and credit union were situated on the edge of a conservative family neighborhood, protestors demonstrated outside. Since I had the gift of gab, I was pushed out the door to confront them. This is what I said: "We only do early terminations. It's not yet a baby. It's just unwanted tissue. We have the right to self-determine. It's our bodies."

A youngish mother with a child listened patiently to my explanation and simply replied, "If it wasn't alive, it wouldn't be growing." She looked down at her little girl, clinging to her mother's hand, and said, "This child was once that small thing you call unwanted tissue. And so was I. So were you."

I flinched, turned on my heal, and marched inside. That reply made me mad. It made too much sense.

A trifecta of events brewed the perfect storm in my life. First of all, my friend Cathy got murdered. She was a sweet young Jewish doctor hired by us to do abortions. She really believed in doing good. Also serving as a doctor at the regional men's prison, she came upon a disturbing discovery there. She found a kilo of heroin in the broom closet of the prison clinic. During this time, she and I were conducting health classes at the women's prison and became close. She worriedly confided in me about the drugs, exclaiming with grief, "I was wondering why so many of my patients had needle marks and were getting hepatitis while incarcerated. I don't know what to do!"

I asked if she did anything with the heroin, and she said she was too scared to do anything with it. I encouraged her to report it. She said she couldn't trust law enforcement. After all, who runs the penal system? So she contacted the local newspaper and arranged for a meeting with a reporter. Cathy was found slumped over the steering wheel of her car on the shoulder of the expressway, with a bullet to the back of her head. The newspaper did not report it.

This so shook me up I could hardly think straight. I stupidly plunged ahead and started asking questions, myself. Some of my friends grew afraid of me and kept their distance, thinking I'd be next.

At the same time, the credit union women decided that the upstairs office they occupied was too small. They lent themselves enough money to buy a multi-story, very old building downtown. Big mistake. They were in over their heads. They couldn't keep up with the repairs. They were taking heat from the authorities. The credit union members staged a rebellion. It turned into a fist fight. A few of them got arrested. That story made it into the newspaper.

While the credit union was collapsing, I was still mulling over that demonstrator's reply about life beginning earlier than I thought. One day I got called to assist the doctor with an abortion. Usually at the woman's head as a counselor, I would coach her to take a deep breath, warn her she'd feel a pinch (from the anesthetic applied to her cervix), and some cramping (when the cannula caused vacuum pressure in her uterus), and so on.

But this particular time, I was at the other end. Which meant I had to transfer the collection jar contents into a container to be sent off to pathology. As I dumped out the bloody substance, I saw tissue, all right. And a tiny hand. And a foot. It was a very early termination. I shook as I labeled the container that obviously held a seven-week broken baby.

Making matters even worse, this was an abortion the girl did not want. Her mother, who practically dragged her in, insisted she have it. As a counselor at a pro-woman-centered facility, I was expected to help each patient identify her needs and desires and encourage her to choose what she thought was best for herself. It didn't work that way this time. The young client clearly stated she wanted to keep the baby and was obviously depressed at the prospect of destroying it. Then why did it go this way? Because the director said that the teenage girl was too young to know what was best for her. Funny, but when parents, who did not want their daughters to get an abortion, tried that argument, they got labeled as abusive and were summarily dismissed.

I was bummed out. So I called Sheila.

"Well, Marney," my friend drawled. "You know, I kinda wondered about what you were doing. It doesn't sound like a very nice way to make a living. Killing babies, and all. If you want to help people, why don't you go into nursing or something nice like that?"

I thought about going back to college for a bare moment, and rejected it. I'd already blown my grade point average and lost the scholarship when I hooked up with Stuart and started working full time. "I just don't know what to do," I whined.

"Ask God," she replied matter-of-factly.

I tried to process this. *How? Ask myself? If I'm God, that is.*

She invited herself over to my apartment to talk later. I put her off and hung up.

I was ready to quit. All the brawling, Cathy's murder, the uncertainty, and the hypocrisy were pushing me out. But to where?

I got in the car, lit up a joint, took one puff, and put it in the ash tray. What the heck. I decided to give it a try.

I asked out loud: "Hey! What's it all about? When does life begin? What happens when I die? Is the world going to blow up? Is there a God? ARE YOU THERE?"

I guess I must have been a little sincere. Because He answered me. Not with a voice in my ears, but in my heart, my inner being, that place I was supposed to be going to in TM.

"I love you. I'm Jesus," was what I got.

Now, let me explain that this short answer did not come alone. It rode on a wave completely filling me with warm liquid love. I'd never experienced anything like it. I was so dumb-founded, I couldn't think how to pursue it. I was immersed in love sweeping over and within me. I just drove automatically and wept. Oh, and I got the shivers. Big time. After all, I'd just heard from God. From Jesus, no less.

I drove straight home and called Sheila. I tried to tell her what happened in the car and how angry I was because of Cathy's murder. She came right over. And brought a Bible.

Now, Sheila is not the talkative type. She just handed me the Bible and said, "Here you go. This should help." After a little while of listening to me complain some more about my present situation, she offered a way out. "Why don't you go out West with John?" Her brother was moving to New Mexico and wanted help with the driving.

I thought that sounded pretty good. Especially if I was next in line to get a bullet in my head. She left. I picked up the Bible, got to the part about Cain killing Abel, and put it down. It was hard to read and made no sense to me whatsoever. Even worse, it did not bring back that extraordinarily wonderful feeling of being loved when I heard from Jesus. Since I was tired and dejected and just wanted to run away, I called John and started packing.

The ride to New Mexico was uneventful. John is pretty boring and wanted to go straight through. So I slept while he drove and vice versa. We arrived on a Friday night and trudged into a house he was to share with a friend. They said I could stay until I figured things out. That didn't take long. I didn't care for their slovenly housekeeping, misogynist comments, and disgusting habits of beer drinking, shooting guns, and whooping it up during TV sports shows. If you could throw a dart at a feminist target, this one hit the bull's eye.

I grabbed a job at a massage parlor. Now, don't be too shocked. I was pretty good at giving massages (learned that in self-help class) and I still regarded men as sex machines. It was the perfect combination. The money was good, and so were the hours. I had the early morning shift from one a.m. to nine a.m. That left my days free. I slept in the early evening and napped between my four to six customers.

The other girls on my shift were nice. One of them invited me to room with her, which solved my housing problem. Judy was carefree. We became best friends. She liked to clean, and I liked to cook. She let me borrow her car. On our days off, we'd camp out with her boyfriend in the desert or mountains. Sometimes he'd bring along another guy, so I'd have a partner, too. That's how I got introduced to peyote.

Chapter 3

Leviticus 19:31 (NIV)

"Do not turn to mediums or seek out spiritists, for you will be defiled by them. I am the Lord your God."

NEW MEXICO IS STEEPED IN NATIVE American culture, which I found fascinating. The terrain proudly discloses a rich and sometimes hidden history, which is especially attractive to those who can relate to the spiritual values of its ancient inhabitants. It is truly the "Land of Enchantment." Exploring remote canyons and multicolored rock striations brought out the artist in me. And the dreamer. I especially loved sleeping out under the crowded canopy of stars, far from city lights and noise. At certain heights, you can gaze out and see an eagle in the air mere yards away. There's nothing quite like the thrill of being eye level with that majestic bird as he coolly observes you while gliding by.

Once, we chanced upon a cave with Indian drawings on the wall. There was something that looked like a turtle and a moon. It was amazing. We worshipped the Great Spirit at this dank, forgotten altar of people long gone. It was here that I became a nature worshipper. And what better way to do that than under the influence of mescaline, the psychedelic drug found in peyote buttons. What really set me up for this kind of spiritual exploration were the books by Carlos Castaneda about the Yaqui Indian way. His stories glorified the mystic shamans who ritualistically took the hallucinogen and communed with spirits, some represented by certain animals.

My spirit guide was a cactus. That's right, a prickly pear, no less. But hold on, first I've gotta tell you about the snake and the bees. We were hiking up a winding, rocky trail with a tattered map of the terrain. Our goal was to ascend to a marked bluff where we would camp that night. Halfway there, we were very low on water and stopped for a break.

The map showed a side trail that split off to a water source. I asked to see the map. We'd gone way too far. So we turned around and began our descent on the slippery, gravel-covered surface. I was second in line when I heard a rattle, and the guy in front of me abruptly stiffened and croaked out, "Snake!" He tried to stop but began to slide, right toward the curled up and poised to strike rattler in the middle of the trail. I sat down, dug in my heels, and grabbed his legs. He dropped down on me. The snake looked at the ridiculous multilimbed creature in disgust, uncurled, and slithered off. We disentangled ourselves, sweating in adrenaline-charged relief, and continued to the obscure side trail. Coming off that we found ourselves in a desert pasture, as evidenced by petrified cow patties. There, by a broken fence, was a pipe coming out of the ground with no spigot. It was slowly going drip, drip, drip. And it was surrounded by a cloud of bees.

We were so thirsty, but we just stood there and studied the perplexing situation. I noticed that the bees were taking turns drinking. So, divinely inspired, I prayed out loud, "Oh Spirit of the bees, please let us take a turn, too." I took off my backpack, slowly edged closer to the pipe, half closed my eyes, and put my head into the bee swarm. They parted, and I drank. Reverently backing up out of the way, the bees again closed in on the water. I looked at my companions, who looked at me, astounded. But eventually, thirst trumped fear, and we all got our fill, topped off the canteens, and proceeded back to the main trail. We suffered not one sting.

After this incident, I was riding high and believed more and more in the spiritual aspect of nature and how important it was for me to be one with all creation. Gingerly stepping past a variety of spiky cacti around the base of a mountain one spring near Truth or Consequences (yes, that's the actual name of a place), I came upon my new mentor. He (she?) was in full bloom. The cactus proudly displayed big, bright orange blossoms and stood at least six feet tall. Very impressive. I was tripping on peyote and slightly nauseated. You see, you have to very carefully scrape away the hairs in the center of the button before consuming it. They contain strychnine. And it's best to have an empty stomach when you eat the bitter fruit. I mean, it's gross. Especially, when it gets crushed and slimy in your pocket.

Anyway, there I was, wandering away from my companions, when I came upon this beautiful behemoth. I stood next to my new spirit guide for a long time and felt a sort of whooshing in my head. Then I heard it: "You have much to learn."

Now, when a prickly pear speaks to you, you'd better listen. So I asked, "What?"

No answer. I was elated for quite a while, just staring at a plant. I'd actually heard from my nature spirit guide! Then I got scared. I was alone in this vast wilderness, and the cactus seemed as indifferent as Stuart. I couldn't see Judy or the guys. I stood rooted to the ground until nearly sunset when they backtracked and found me. It was getting cold on the desert floor. Judy led me to where they'd set up camp. I don't think I slept at all that night. I just sat on my sleeping bag, bundled in a blanket, looking around at the night sky and listening to whispers on the wind. I perceived the presence of other beings, descending and circling around me. Was that a poke in my back? It gave me the creeps, and I trembled with fear. Nature could also be very dangerous. And there was something unseen pricking me. I never did peyote again.

A few weeks later, Judy and I decided to take a yoga class. Now, this was a natural next step for me. It combined body movement, meditation, and Eastern mysticism, which seemed to me to be not that much different than tripping out in nature. The various postures were named after animals and gods. As I got good at it, I felt like I was invoking the nature and character of each entity the posture called for. The philosophy was to become one with the universe. I recalled how the cactus made me feel, well, somehow related to creation. Like a distant cousin, maybe. These exercises kind of did the same thing, by opening me up to spiritual awareness. I began painting sunsets and mountains and cacti in vivid color from memory. I also got pretty flexible and lost that weight. Things were going great.

But when the yoga instructor got deeper into the meaning and goal of yoga, I became confused again. He said that the ultimate was to achieve Nirvana, or nothingness. Nothingness? Now, that didn't appeal to me one bit. Sure, I wanted to be free of suffering. But I wanted more. I wanted to achieve somethingness. Where was the love I felt when Jesus answered me? I grew uncomfortable with the class. Judy dropped her boyfriend and started dating the instructor. He moved in with us. So I had to move out.

I was also ready to quit the massage parlor. It was because one night, three Arab men came in, which was fine with me. I had no prejudice about race or color or anything. A man was a man, that's all. But the one who came back with me was disrespectful and got rough. He tried to force me. I punched him in the nose and ran out the room. Our bodyguard told them to leave. But the incident turned my stomach.

I called Sheila.

"Have you been reading your Bible?" she asked.

"Bible!" I exclaimed. "Sheila, I don't know what to do. And that Bible you gave me got left behind when I came out here."

"Oh," she said. "Well, that's okay. I'll send you another one."

I wanted to scream. I repeated that things were kind of falling apart for me in New Mexico. With her usual calm, Sheila listened patiently and then offered a solution. "So why don't you come back here? You can stay with me and my folks until you get it together."

Stay with her folks? I'd just as soon stay with my own, which would be awful. I was used to my free spirited, wild ways. I sadly reviewed my present circumstances, and concluded that, come to think of it, going home actually sounded pretty good. So I bought a plane ticket and started packing.

Chapter 4

2 Timothy 4:3–4 (NIV)

"For the time will come when people will not put up with sound doctrine. Instead, to suit their own desires, they will gather around them a great number of teachers to say what their itching ears want to hear. They will turn their ears away from the truth and turn aside to myths."

I ARRIVED AT MY HOME AIRPORT, STASHED my suitcase in a locker, and went outside to get some exercise and fresh air. Sheila said she'd pick me up after work. While I was killing time, I was approached by a clean-shaven young man wearing a ball cap, neat khakis, and a T-shirt that had a smiling, black face on it with huge eyes and a ring in the spot where there should've been a nose. I asked him about the cartoonish character he was wearing, and he beamed at me. He said it was God, called Lord Jagannatha. Then he handed me a flower and a card out of his shoulder bag and asked me where I was going. I told him a little about my seeking spiritual truth, thinking I might enlighten him.

What I did was give him an open door. He lit up, handed me a book, and said, "If you really want to know the absolute truth, you need to read this. It's the essence of all knowledge from ancient India."

I took the book and studied the cover. On it was a blue, bare-chested male figure wearing an elaborate crown and flower garland,

16

seated on a chariot pulled by white horses. Bowing before him with folded hands was another man, also crowned and garlanded. The name *Bhagavad Gita, the Song of God* was blazoned across the thick, beautifully bound hardback.

Still talking, the man said that this book would answer all my questions and was mine for a donation. I looked up from the colorful back cover, which showed an elderly Indian man seated on a wide fancy chair and almost obliterated by numerous garlands around his neck.

"How much?" I asked, reaching for my wallet.

He peaked into my purse and said that the more I gave, the more I'd be blessed. This book was worth my entire life. So I found myself handing him a hundred dollar bill.

He beckoned to a young woman standing off to the side and watching us. She was wearing a long paisley patterned cotton skirt and shawl with foreign lettering on it. She introduced herself as Bhakti and asked if I'd ever visited the Krishna temple. I said no. She asked where I was going. My muddled brain told me to say, "I don't know."

That's how I wound up in a van with a party of Krishna book distributors headed back to their temple.

Sheila called. "Where are you?"

"Oh," I said. "I'm with the devotees at the temple."

"What temple? I'm here at the airport looking for you," she replied, sounding bewildered. "Did you make it back okay?"

I explained what happened at the airport, apologized, and hung up.

My indoctrination into the movement progressed with rapid intensity. Everyone was so nice. With my suitcase on the tiled floor in the corner of a large room, I surveyed my new home. It was bare, except for a pile of bed rolls along one wall and a full bookshelf along another wall. Bhakti took me to the dining hall, where I was instructed to sit down on the floor between two other women. The room was full of barefoot devotees. On one side sat the men with shaven heads (except for a patch on their pate like a ponytail). Veiled women sat across from them, all in rows. One of the men began to sing a song in a language I'd never heard. The others joined in. Then they all dipped forward, touching their heads to the floor, mumbled something unintelligible, rocked back on their fannies, and exclaimed, "Jaya!"

Several young male initiates, called brahmacharis, proceeded to pass out paper plates, cups, and spoons. Next, pushing big white buckets along the floor, they ladled out vegetarian preparations and a fruit drink. I was hungry, and the food was delicious.

By now, I knew that the elderly Indian gentleman was not only the author of the book I bought, he was the revered founder of this movement. He traveled from India to New York City in the 1960s and quickly became a draw for young seekers of that generation, eventually including such notables as one of the Beatles.

They kept a strict schedule. Everyone was up by three-thirty in the morning to attend worship at four. Then came chanting on beads from five-thirty to seven, another worship service followed by breakfast at nine, work for the temple all day until worship after dinner at seven, and finally, read the devotional books until lights out by nine!

But I did it and became an official brahmacarini, female celibate devotee. At first, they had me making flower garlands for the deities standing on the altar. These manifestations of Krishna and other associates of his were worshiped as God. As Bhakti explained, "These are not idols. We practice serving God in his authorized deity form so that we can be good at it when we join him after we leave our bodies."

She sounded so sure of this, like God could really be an artistically created metal object. I wondered if I became really good at this thing, maybe I could become one of Krishna's girlfriends after quitting this world.

Although rigorously disciplined, I was actually enjoying this lifestyle. They kept me so busy, I had no time to think about my problems. It was refreshingly different. I liked the flowers and incense. I liked wearing the pretty saris they gave me. The other women were sweet and kind. Yes, a thin bedroll on the floor was hard, but I'd be so tired by the time I lay down, I didn't mind too much.

Chapter 5

Mathew 6:7 (NIV)

"When you pray, don't babble on and on as the Gentiles do. They think their prayers are answered merely by repeating their words again and again."

EVERYTHING WAS GOING ALONG PRETTY smoothly, until we heard that a guru was coming to visit. That threw everyone into a highly organized tizzy. At this point, according to the rules of disciplic succession, the guru was a spiritual descendant of the founder, who had passed away some years earlier. Because I had an interest in cooking, they assigned me to the huge kitchen. It was hard, hot work, but I loved it. I was learning so much about vegetarian preparations with Indian spices.

The devotees in the kitchen mostly got along with one another. Mostly. This annoying, arrogant brahmachari, named Nimai, would sometimes be conscripted to help out when we were in a pinch. You see, the meals served to the deities had to be *exactly* on time. If the head of the kitchen wanted to, he could pull another person in to chop, stir, or fry. Since I didn't have the second initiation necessary to be able to actually cook, all I could do was wash, cut, grind, or do anything else in prep. But Nimai buddy boy had the thread over his chest to prove he had that super second endorsement from Krishna allowing one to use fire. He enjoyed giving me a hard time. I did my best to ignore his disparaging remarks about my being a neophyte, less intelligent woman who didn't even have the first initiation yet.

The morning of the guru's anticipated arrival, I was sent with a bucket of soapy water to his ashram (a little cottage on the grounds) to help other women clean. We were almost done when my companions left to get flowers and cushions. I was alone, bareheaded with the veil tucked into my waist and mopping when the door flung open. Suddenly, the notable one was there, frowning at me.

After only a slight hesitation, this short, bespectacled, middle-aged man in perfectly pressed silk saffron robes strode in accompanied by several young men importantly carrying his things. The temple president walked over to me and hissed, "Bow down." I jerked the veil out of the waistband, trying to cover my disheveled hair. The dirty sari unraveled. I grabbed the mess of material and hit the wet floor to mutter my obeisances. The guru pretended to ignore my disgraceful self. The temple president told me to take the bucket and get out. I was humiliated.

I encountered the other women on the walk through the landscaped courtyard of the temple complex. They were horrified that I had been in the guru's presence unauthorized. I stammered that it wasn't my fault. He came early. They brushed past me and I watched as they handed the cushions and flowers at the door to the brahmacharis serving him. Evidently, women, especially messy ones, were not allowed in the room when the celibate sannyasi guru was in residence.

Shaken, I went to the women's ashram where my things were, sat on my bed roll, and leaned against the wall, weeping. The head mataji (mother) came in to me and consoled me. She explained the etiquette around the guru. Women could be in his presence only at his summoning or congregationally during worship. She knelt down beside me, gave a little hug, suggested I get a shower, change into a nice fresh sari, and chant until it was time for the evening service.

Now, about the chanting, here's the thing. It's done out loud on 108 beads, each representing one of Krishna's girlfriends. It takes a while to go 16 times around all those beads, fingering each one while saying the short mantra. I was behind on my rounds, so I was glad for the chance to be alone and get myself back on track. Instead of trying not to think while meditating, I was taught to pray for Krishna to please engage me in his devotional service while saying his names over and over again.

Try to understand. I really thought that this was God. I repeated the mantra on each bead, around and around for over an hour. As I walked back and forth, fingering the wooden beads, I alternately thought of what an idiot I must have seemed to this holy man, and why on earth should I be upset? I really did try to include that part about praying to do devotional service. It wasn't easy.

I also probably need to explain that, on the flight home, I did some deep soul searching. I knew I needed to change my ways. I was out of control and getting nowhere. I needed discipline, of which I had practically none. I vowed that I was going to be celibate. I'd had so many men, that sex no longer held any meaning or pleasure for me. I made it through the last few promiscuous years without getting pregnant, raped, or seriously diseased. It was time to quit. I also felt the need to be drug free and clear headed. But what would fill my need for attention, for love? Where was that Jesus love I had experienced? Could I ever find it again?

Stumbling upon the devotees at the airport came at a vulnerable time. They were my new family, my home and purpose. I still wanted the answers I'd asked that day after leaving the abortion clinic. The idea of reincarnation partially addressed what happens after death. We get reborn. But as what? A worm? A dog? A human? On which planet? Clearly, the purpose of life is to serve God. As to where God was, well, he was supposedly here on the altar, where he could be fed, worshipped, put to bed at night, and wakened in the morning, like a transcendental doll.

When I mentioned Jesus to one of the leaders, he said that Jesus was a recognized guru for that time and place. But He only had so much to offer those simple fishermen back then. Here, at the temple, I would get the highest truth, so much better than the Bible. That placated me, especially when he said that I was too intelligent to be satisfied with the Christian scripture. Sure, Jesus offered some nice moral instruction. But worshipping Him would only get me to Jesus's planet, at best. Wouldn't it be much more preferable to achieve Krishna's planet, the highest destination, after this lifetime? All I had to do was perform every single devotional service completely perfectly. And work, work, work!

I'd need to follow this religion diligently, not missing a worship service, chanting all my rounds and not committing any sins. With all that in my head, I wondered if I'd come back as a rabbit or a pigeon. Could I ever do enough chanting to unravel all my bad karma? I was willing to try.

While the guru was visiting, I got called into the temple president's office. Not knowing what to expect, I was a little nervous and pulled the veil part of the sari tightly around my face. His proposal surprised me.

"How would you like to get initiated?" he asked. Then, without waiting for me to answer, he continued to tell me that the guru didn't come here very often and I should take advantage of his mercy and ask to become his disciple. He advised me that it was necessary to have a guru to intervene for me spiritually. This would require a formality known as a fire sacrifice, during which I would vow to follow regulative principles for the rest of my life. My guru, in turn, would spiritually guide me by accepting service from me (read: money). I thought it sounded good and agreed to it. He sent me off to write a personal note to the man, explaining a little about myself and why I wanted to be his disciple.

Two nights later, dressed in a borrowed silk sari, I sat cross-legged before a small container in the middle of the temple floor. Instead of wood, the fire was fueled by clarified butter, or ghee. I swore to abstain from illicit sex, intoxication, gambling and eating meat, fish, and eggs. I also promised to chant at least 16 rounds of the mantra every day. Guruji accepted me. I threw some rice into the fire. From his high cushioned chair, he pronounced my new name, Devahuti devi dasi.

Hindu names have meaning. The character, Devahuti, was written of in the ancient Indian scriptures, called the Vedas, and purported to be actual histories. She was said to be the daughter of a king, given in marriage to a great wiseman. The devi dasi part simply meant that I was her servant. So I sought to learn more about her character. She was virtuous and honorable and became the mother of Krishna in one of his incarnations. Pretty elevated stuff; I congratulated myself proudly.

How many clues does it take to inform me of my mistake? One balmy day during Guruji's visit, us disciples sat on the lawn around his seat as he recited a story from the Vedic literature. Violently, he lurched and screamed in fear, "A bee! I just got stung" he gasped. "Ow ow ow!"

Group tizzy prevailed as young men in saffron robes looked on helplessly while he writhed and clutched the offended arm. I, the only woman present, sat a distance behind to witness this ridiculous chaos. Asked if he was allergic, he just said, "I don't know. But it hurts like hell!"

I calmly walked to the kitchen, grabbed a box of baking soda and a glass of water, made a paste, and handed it to a brahmachari, who glared at my humble self and barked, "What's that for?"

"Just put it on his arm," I said and walked back to my ashram, pondering disappointment. If this guy was so spiritual and powerful, why was he freaking out? Why didn't he just take charge of his flesh and command the pain to go? Or at least tolerate it like any good monk. And why on earth didn't he have a better relationship with the bee spirits?

Despite this leader's apparent flaw, I still wanted to believe in the infallibility of God's truth as proposed in this movement. I really thought I had found it. But certain elements of our past practices stick when we try something new. They just kinda morph into a new form. I later realized this cult wasn't a totally new beginning for me. It was a continuation of my thus far accumulated repertoire. The true new beginning would come later.

It was about this time that Sheila contacted me through the temple office, wanting to know if I was okay. Someone fetched me to take the call. Standing before the secretary, I told Sheila that I was in bliss and invited her to the Sunday feast. I explained it was when many guests come to enjoy the beautiful worship ceremony and the delicious food, which I helped to prepare. I returned the phone to the cradle and got an approving nod from the watchful witness behind his desk.

Sheila came. She was quietly observant during the visit and only asked a few questions. Mostly, I talked. I wanted her to understand how wonderful everything was. I hoped that maybe she could become a devotee, too. Chances of that seemed pretty slim when she took me aside and said, "Marney, you can call me any time, and I'll come get you." She looked worried, gave me a hug, and drove off.

I shrugged off Sheila's attitude and went back inside to dance and chant in front of the deities some more. The next day, Guruji left and I was back to the well-ordered routine of temple life—until the president sent for me again. This time, it was a proposal I was not at all happy about.

"It's time for you to get married," he said. He wasn't smiling, and neither was I.

Chapter 6

Ephesians 5:25 (NIV)

"Husbands, love your wives, just as Christ loved the church and gave Himself up for her."

HERE'S THE SHOCKER: NOT ONLY WAS MY temple president telling me to get married, the husband picked out for me was none other than, yep, you guessed it, Nimai the Nuisance.

I suppose that, in my silent alarm at practically being ordered to marry, the temple president must have taken my nonresponse as agreement. But when he told me who he had in mind for me, I may have offended him some. "NO!" I screeched.

He blinked, sat back, and regrouped, addressing me by a respectful term for a woman that means "mother." "Now, mataji," he soothed, "Nimai is a very advanced devotee, and he has asked specifically for you." He thought that would please me.

I wanted to ask the thirtyish man trying to dictate my life if he was crazy. Instead, I just told him about my negative encounters with the candidate.

He replied that poor Nimai was just "agitated" and was having difficulty maintaining his celibate state. Therefore, he probably just acted out of frustration, and (the TP was trying to be delicate) need. But Nimai must really like me, and that's why he might have seemed a little less than respectful at times.

What I heard in this little speech was none other than weasel words. Before dropping out of college, I took some classes in communication, advertising, and journalism. I can recognize a smarmy sales pitch when I hear one.

I folded my arms across my chest and replied, "Absolutely not."

Unaccustomed to rebellion, the TP stood up, leaned over with hands on hips, and dropped the guru bomb.

"Devahuti," he intoned authoritatively, "Guruji has given his approval for this match. He is the representative of God and knows things you do not. Do you really think you can disobey your spiritual master and please Krishna?"

I tell you truly, this is where I should have just run out of there, screaming. But I no longer had cell phone service. I couldn't call Sheila. All I could do was try and damp down the panic in my chest, turn on my heel, and march out of there. I went straight to the temple room. The altar curtain was closed, shutting off the deities. It was their nap time. So I plunked down on the floor, head to the ground, before the statue of the founding guru that we worshipped at the far end of the room. There I sat. I didn't know how to pray for deliverance or peace. I expected some kind of help to come from this life-like figure on a raised seat, dressed in silk and wearing a wilting necklace of marigolds. I got nothing.

After a while, I wiped my eyes, arose, and began walking toward my ashram, not knowing where else I could go in my misery and confusion.

"Devahuti, wait," came from behind. I turned and saw Nimai. He was wearing white, indicating he was ready to become a householder. He smiled.

There's something about a smile that changes one's face. Nimai had attractive blue eyes when he smiled. Before, they had seemed icy. Actually, he was pretty good-looking, tall, square shouldered, and trim.

No doubt my eyes were red and my down-turned mouth could hardly form a word. I just stared at him, slump shouldered and feeling small.

He took a few steps closer, indicated a decorative cement bench along the flower-bordered walkway. I sat down at one end. He sat at the other.

For the first time in my adult life, I felt shy around a man. On the trip back from New Mexico, when I resolved to change my ways, I made a vow to the Great Spirit, God, Jesus, Universal Whatever, declaring that from then on, I was going to lay off sex until I got married. I was done with promiscuity and launched myself in the opposite direction. I wanted to be a virgin, again. Please don't laugh. I longed for the innocence I had trampled over in my teens. I know you can't un-ring a bell. But in my mind, I was going to see myself as a virgin and conduct myself accordingly.

Nimai cleared his throat. "The temple president said he talked to you," he looked at me intently and made me blush.

I wondered if the TP told Nimai what I said. Evidently not, because after a short pause, Nimai continued. "He suggested that we have a wedding fire sacrifice while some of the visiting sannyasis are still in town."

Heat crept up my neck. I blinked. Suddenly, it started to rain. I jumped up and sprinted to the women's ashram without saying a word, practically tripping on the hem of my sodden cotton sari.

By the time I got through the door to the sleeping room, I was in full panic. Bhakti was there, sewing buttons on a choli, the little top worn under a sari. She looked up from her work and smiled at me. "You're soaked," she clucked.

After changing, I approached the head mother and was about to tell her what was going on, when she held up the choli.

"I'm moving the buttons for you," she said. It was then that I noticed that this was not an ordinary choli. Gold-threaded embroidery decorated the edges of the short sleeves and around the neck. The buttons were gold, too. Next to Bhakti was a folded crimson sari, so elaborately woven with golden stitching that it was stiff.

I looked at her inquiringly, and she explained, "I'm giving you my wedding sari. I've only worn it once. I thought that, since you're smaller than me, all I needed to do was move the buttons. Do you like it?" she held it up by the shoulder seams and beamed.

"How did you know? I mean, I didn't even say I'd get married!" I was flabbergasted.

"Oh, every girl wants to get married," she replied matter-of-factly. "My husband told me about it last night after evening worship."

Bhakti was Mrs. TP and evidently party to this conspiracy to end my newfound virginity. I sat down next to her, sighed, and said it was beautiful. It was the kind of opulent material from India that they made the deities' clothes out of. As I looked at it and thought about Nimai's eyes, and the TP explaining why Nimai had acted as such a jerk, I felt myself softening. I'd just vowed to follow, to surrender, to submit to this spiritual culture. Maybe, just maybe, this wouldn't be a bad idea, after all.

Chapter 7

Ephesians 4:25 (NIV)

"Therefore, each of you must put off falsehood and speak truthfully to your neighbor, for we are all members of one body."

OUR RUSHED WEDDING HAD BEEN QUITE an experience. Another fancy fire sacrifice before the deities in which we vowed to remain faithful to Krishna and each other was followed by a feast. I didn't have time to invite my family or Sheila. To my surprise, I continued to sleep in the women's ashram, and Nimai stayed in the brahmachari ashram. There were no householder rooms available. I wondered how my "agitated" husband was coping. We had barely even had a conversation, let alone kissed. So a "virgin" bride I remained—until the temple president called us into his office.

"My wife and I are traveling to LA for a meeting, and you two can use our apartment while we're gone," he announced. "But in three days, I want you to come out to LA, as well. Here are your tickets," he reached into a desk drawer and handed Nimai an envelope.

Nimai seemed nonplussed. I was at sea.

"Since you're both experienced in the printing business, Krishna and guruji are engaging you in doing service for our movement's newspaper out there," he explained, mostly to me.

Evidently, Nimai already knew about this. I could tell he was chomping at the bit the way he was nodding and smiling and saying, "Jaya prabhu!" (Read: Oh boy!)

You didn't know this, but my former job back home, before the abortion clinic, was in a print shop. I'd told Bhakti about it and that I'd taken some college courses in writing and journalism. I didn't dare mention anything about my exploits in New Mexico or much else about my history.

Nimai's regular service at the temple was in the office, producing a local newsletter and creating contacts with the Hindu Indians in our area so that they would attend special temple holiday functions and give donations.

Would you believe that we got the entire day off of service the next day? Of course, Nimai and I still had to attend all the temple worship. But we were excused from doing anything else because we were going to be in that apartment by ourselves. And it takes about six hours to chant 50 rounds. That's right, folks, 50 times around on those 108 beads is what you have to chant before having sex with your spouse. And let me tell, after chanting 50 rounds, the last thing you feel like doing is having sex. Or so I thought. But not so with my husband. He ripped through those rounds like a house on fire. As I was finishing up, he went to the main temple kitchen to get us something to eat, which sat on a table in the apartment for another two hours.

The next morning, I slept in. When Nimai shook me awake around 3:00, I lied and told him he wore me out. That made him happy. He went to the temple service without me. I lay there alone and imagined him trying to fake humility, but actually gloating before the brahmacharis of his manly conquest. He'd clang his brass caratalas and loudly sing the same old prescribed Sanskrit song before the deities at four in the morning in his usual spot, right up front by the altar. Truly comfortable for the first time in months, I luxuriously stretched out over the whole full-size futon and slept till seven.

Much had happened by four days later. When I woke in the middle of the night with a start from a bad dream in the LA women's quarters, pain shot through my back. My body protested the cement floor beneath the thin mat they gave me in the crowded room. It was too early to rise for first worship. But, after four tortuous nights, I could not lay down on that thing anymore. I looked around, got oriented, and quietly showered. Even that was no comfort. The floor felt slimy, and the water stayed cold. Walking outside in the dark with my beads, but not chanting, I recalled a part of the nightmare. It was one of those freaky bathroom dreams where I couldn't find a private, clean place to relieve myself. There was something else about it, too. I clearly remembered hearing, "Love truth, hate lies." What was that about?

The temple compound, situated over two city blocks and surrounded by poor neighborhoods and ethnic groceries, seemed forebodingly eerie at that hour. By the time, I got back to the room where the women slept; many had already gone to the temple. I lingered, not really wanting to go. What disturbed me, besides the dream, was the meeting Nimai and I sat in the day before. A panel of leaders grilled us about being committed to doing the newspaper. It was there I discovered that my husband had been in the Marines, and discharged with PTSD after serving in Afghanistan. Why was this important to them? The VA gave him disability pay, and that was the real reason we were chosen for this service. As householders, we would be financially responsible for doing the newspaper!

Nimai was eager to take on this great honor. I was scared. I knew the costs of printing. When I asked the panel about housing, one of the leaders replied, "Isn't that just like a woman, to think of her own comfort, first?" He didn't even make eye contact with me. Shame made my face feel hot.

Anyway, I was about to trudge over to the temple this morning, when Lila, one of the women sharing the room, approached me. She was a cook and a "widow" (read: her husband abandoned her for the higher calling of celibate preaching). Lila was in her late thirties, had swollen legs from standing barefoot for hours on a hard kitchen floor, and wore a stained, white sari, denoting her austere widow-hood. She bowed down before me, her head to the floor, and said, "Please accept my obeisances. You are a great devotee to be entrusted with Krishna's sacred newspaper."

I must have been desperate for something supportive about the situation because my heart swelled at the words of a truly humble person. So I walked with this devoted servant to the temple. I rarely got to talk with gentle Lila after that bit of encouragement, however. Life got *very* busy.

It was about ten at night a couple of weeks later, and I was still typesetting the 24-page tabloid, racing toward a deadline, when my husband came into the cramped office space designated for our use. Working in the basement of the building, which housed the prestigious book publishing operation, I sometimes felt like the orphaned cousin. He brought me a bite to eat and suggested I come to bed. At this point, Nimai and I were finally moved up to a room in the householders' quarters. I ate a little but set it aside, not wanting to gain all the weight I'd lost in New Mexico. He helped me shut everything down, and we walked the short distance to our place.

On the way, I asked him why he hadn't told me about his disability award from the VA. He said he didn't want me to marry him for his money. Like, right, that would have been the deciding factor. I was actually more interested in the reason for the disability. And besides, shouldn't married people openly discuss their finances?

Then, he asked me why I consented to marry him. I wondered when had I actually consented. Instead of waiting for me to formulate an answer, he posed the big question.

"Have you ever been with a man, before?" he asked as he opened the door.

I walked in behind him and fished around for a plausible reply. "Well, yes, I had a boyfriend back in Florida. But that was a long time ago."

That got a grunt and a frown out of him. I silently petitioned the Lord, "Oh, God, no more questions!" I sure as shootin' wasn't going to ask him *anything* more about his private life. Had he killed people in Afghanistan? Did he see his buddies die in horrible explosions? He was kinda jumpy and had a hair-trigger temper, which I was learning to circumvent. Did he need anger management classes? What would he do to me if he knew how promiscuous I'd been?

He shed his clothes and climbed into bed. Then I got a brilliant idea and said, "Before I married you, I decided to be celibate until I found God and a husband." Since that was somewhat true, it came across as genuine and seemed to put him at ease. Either that, or Nimai had already tuned out. He started snoring.

Months went by, one newspaper edition at a time. It was challenging and interesting. Although Nimai and I did all the production and fulfillment work, we were overseen by a panel of highly placed muckity mucks. They gave no financial support but dictated what we could and could not print. Sometimes this irritated me. They wanted the headline stories to tout the elite leaders' activities. I preferred to feature stories about the ordinary devotees who did neat things. Like the one about the brahmachari in San Francisco who every morning would load up a white bucket of kicheri (a spiced combo of rice, Asian beans, and vegetables) onto his skateboard and feed the homeless.

Things began to unravel when I received a story that would blow the bosses heads off *if* we printed it. It was from a former student in one of their schools. You see, when members had children, the kids were separated at about age five and sent to live in the movement's schools to be groomed as great devotees, able to convert the world. Incidentally, that freed the parents to go out and do more collecting and other devotional service for the movement.

Well, tragically, wherever there are children, child molesters infiltrate, unless the institution is wise and vigilant. This one was not.

I read the story and broke into a sweat. Was it real? Then I got another one. And another one. Having learned from my past about investigating a lead, I was careful. The alleged victims arranged to meet me secretly. A flood of testimonies and a couple of ex-teachers came forward. It was real. The movement's schools were a cesspool of abuse and molestation.

The next edition was all set, approved by the band of bosses. The day we had to send it to the printer, an advertiser pulled out. That left a quarter of a page empty. How to fill it? I looked my notes and quotes over from the secret meeting and went to work.

When Nimai came in to check on me, since it was my job to finalize the last proof before press, he noticed my furious typing and asked what I was doing. I quickly minimized the screen and faked a yawn. I knew he wouldn't let me run anything that would make the movement look bad. The paper went to members and donors all over the world. He would never buck the big boys. Oh, but I would. In fact, I really wanted to. So I lied and told him I'd already uploaded the paper to the printer and I was just composing a letter. He said to get home soon. I climbed into bed with him three hours later.

Chapter 8

Matthew 18:10 (NIV)

"See that you do not despise one of these little ones.
For I tell you that their angels in heaven always see
the face of my Father in heaven."

HAVE YOU EVER SUCKER PUNCHED
someone? Well, that's pretty much what I did to the leaders I was
beginning to despise. I just didn't realize how much I resented their
arrogance until I hit that final key that sent the publication to the
printer. Oh! The thrill of rebellion tastes sweet indeed! But was I
ready for the stormy reaction?

The results of the article, placed in the least seen part of the
paper, the inner bottom corner of page 16, were cataclysmic. The
enraged leaders commanded Nimai to dump me after he pleaded
that he had no clue of what I'd been up to. The movement's lawyers
frantically met with top gurus and spiritual big wigs to do damage
control. Second generation devotees came forward in droves with
their horror stories. Surprisingly, only a few of their parents hired
lawyers. How could so many be silent? They'd been brainwashed,
that's how. They feared their overseers more than they felt outraged
by the big betrayal. But not the kids. Oh, no! They organized, and
the legal battle began.

I actually asked some parents who were defensive with me, why
they didn't come out swinging. Sure enough, they feared getting

kicked out of the society. It seemed to me they'd become somewhat desensitized about their children because of the unnatural culture of separating family members. This made me mad. Most of these rank-and-file devotees were sweet, sincere, and trusting people. Unfortunately, they bought the lie that spreading the movement was more important than raising their children. So they handed their kids over to be properly indoctrinated. Hey, didn't Hitler's Nazi society do that?

The newspaper suffered imminent demise. Temples that paid for bulk orders and advertisers defected. Subscriptions among the Indian community dropped off. Nimai, who had just gone in rather heavy debt to buy new computers, was facing bankruptcy.

Later that tense week, I walked into the huge kitchen, wearing one of Lila's worn white saris. The head cook barked at me to wash pots. These are really big, heavy pots and woks. But I went to work, blinking back tears streaming from my black eye. Before reporting for my severely demoted devotional duty that morning, Nimai let me have it. As he coiled up his fist, he hissed, "Two things get better with beating, a mridanga (drum) and a wife." That happened when I went back to the apartment to get my things. I wanted to strike back, but something told me to get out fast. I left my books and clothes.

You could say that my confidence was at an all-time low. This was worse than civil war among the feminists. I was about to be homeless in a big, strange city. I was far from home, penniless and friendless.

Except for Sheila.

That night, I cried myself to sleep in the women's ashram. In the middle of the night, I got up to pee in the less than clean bathroom. When I lay back down on that awful, thin mat, I started to pray to God to save me. I heard this in my inner being: "I created you to be joyful."

That's it? Well, I wanted my joy; if that's what God wanted, so did I!

I gathered enough change lying around to walk to the 24-hour corner store and ask the friendly proprietor if I could pay to use his phone. He took one look at me, handed me his phone, and pushed the money back to me.

Sheila's an early riser, and it was around seven in the morning her time. She answered the first ring.

"I've been praying for you," she greeted me.

While the Indian man behind the counter listened, I told Sheila what had happened. She softly offered to pay my fare back home. "I've been waiting for your call," my friend declared. "It'll be all right. Jesus loves you, and so do I."

I wiped my nose with my wrist after handing the man's phone back to him. He reached into his pocket, and pulled a 20 from his wallet. "You're a very brave young lady," he said, and smiled. Later that day, I went back to the store to retrieve the Western Union money order Sheila sent. By day's end, I sat in LAX, waiting for my flight.

Sitting at the gate was a déjà vu encounter. What had I done to myself this time? Another wrong turn to another dead end. I really didn't know anything. I intended the truth to come out and help those kids. I later found out that the leadership addressed the victims' cases by raising lots of money that successfully bought a number of them off. They also instituted appropriate standards for teachers in their schools. However, to their shame, they did not pursue criminal charges against the perpetrators, most of whom where well respected and a few highly placed in the echelon. One was even a guru! Instead, they moved them to temples in other countries.

Finally, back in Florida, Sheila greeted me with a big hug. She took a quick look at my hair coming out of its braid, the long Indian paisley skirt dragging on the floor, and the black eye, and softly cooed, "Oh, Marney, it's so good to see you."

It was just like Sheila to look past the mess and simply see me. I broke down.

"Now, now," she coddled. "You're here now. Are you hungry?"

I nodded as I blubbered. She asked if I had baggage. I shook my head no and tried to control my crying. I hiccupped and looked into my friend's face. Love reflected back. I remembered what Jesus said the day I left the abortion clinic. He didn't condemn me or call me a baby killer. All He said was, "I love you." All Sheila did was show deep caring as watery hazel eyes searched my own miserable green peepers. She didn't call me a stupid idiot, which I was. She just took my hand and sweetly guided me to the next chapter of my life. I was ready. This time, I was going to look for God in a person. His name is Jesus.

Chapter 9

Psalm 133:1 (KJV)

"Behold, how good and how pleasant it is for brethren to dwell together in unity!"

IF YOU DON'T HAVE A LOT OF EXPERI-ence with Christianity, you might think, "Oh, end of story. She found Jesus."

But it's not that quick. When you look at the meaning of spirit, it's eternal. So the story just keeps evolving and growing. Look at it this way, every day the sun rises. But every sunrise is different. It comes up at a different point of the horizon as it cycles through the seasons. The clouds and colors are never quite the same. That's the way I see it, anyways.

So when I moved into Sheila's cute two-bedroom condo, I was only just beginning my excursion into life as a Christian. She had a good job as a physical therapist. While I was traipsing around, talking to cacti and worshipping idols, Sheila was getting an education. Her life showcased no drama: church on Sunday, work during the week, laundry and shopping on Saturday. Plus, she was engaged to the youth pastor at church, an even-tempered, pleasant man well suited to my friend. Paul was also a plumber. He'd come over to our place on weekends for dinner. Always the gentleman, he'd bring flowers or some other gift. We never suffered a leaky pipe or clogged toilette. The place was clean and neat and smelled good. I especially liked the way Paul made great eye contact and listened like he genuinely cared. He even did the dishes.

As I commented to Sheila, "Boy, it sure is nice to have a man who knows how to fix things!" And that coming from a former feminist who thought men were good for only—never mind.

The best part about Sheila's condo was that it had a pool and a large garden patio. I loved sitting out there, reading and relaxing. I found a job, too. At first, I took care of an elderly lady in the complex. She liked my cooking. Word got around, and soon I had two more clients there. Lots of retired people live in Florida and many of them prefer to stay in their own homes as long as possible. That's where a reliable caregiver like me comes in. I was able to pay Sheila back for the bailout from LA and carry my share of the expenses. I still didn't have a car. But I didn't need one, either. Sheila and I drove together to church and the store. Plus, I could use my client's car to shop for her and the others. Things were good.

"I'm so happy you're here with me, Marney," Sheila said one evening after Paul left. "Before you came, Paul and I went out to dinner. Now, we can just be together here, and it's so much nicer."

I noticed that Paul never spent the night. When I asked Sheila about that, she said it wouldn't be right for them to be alone at the condo. It might tempt them. It was at that point that it really sunk in. Sheila was sexually pure, just as I longed to be after leaving New Mexico.

In her usual thoughtful way, Sheila picked up on my remorse. "You know, Marney, when you become born again, Jesus takes away all your sin, and you become a new person in Him. The past is gone. Maybe you can talk to my pastor to get more perspective on your life. He's really easy to talk with, and I promise he won't judge you."

You see, the more I spent time with Sheila, the more my shortcomings glared back at me, accusing and convicting. Although I was going to church with her, I didn't think I was born again. I felt rotten about my past. The present was much better. But what about the future? Where was I headed? I hated to admit to myself that I was jealous of my friend and felt guilty about it. I decided to try her pastor. Why not? I'd inquired into other ideas about the God question and my identity. I needed to figure this out, and I sure didn't want to tell Sheila, such a great friend, that I envied her. It was starting to stress me out.

I called Pastor Rick's office and made an appointment. The church Sheila and Paul attended was different from the one she used to go to with her parents. I guess you could say it was less traditional and more upbeat. As Paul described it, this church was Bible based, full gospel, and filled with the Holy Ghost! I liked the teaching because I could understand it, and the contemporary praise and worship songs were exhilarating. There was nothing rigid or ritualistic like the routine, always repeat the same stuff, worship at the Hindu temple. Here was freedom. Sometimes people would spontaneously start to worship. But it didn't feel chaotic, either. Things flowed in a joyful, peaceful way.

Even though the pastor always had a prepared sermon, he was pretty fluid and open to however the spirit was leading. He'd call people to the front and lay hands on them and pray. I liked that. It was personal. And I was learning about how to let go and trust God there. So I figured I might trust this pastor, too. At least, I hoped so. After all, he was just a man. I'd been pretty burned up to now. But I had to try, you know?

I was surprised to be led into a small, cozy living room next to the church office. Pastor Rick and his wife, Donna, both greeted me with a hug. I sat on the cushy light blue chair opposite them on the matching couch. I was offered coffee.

Pastor Donna started the conversation, asking me how I knew Sheila. I told them we'd been friends since we were kids in school.

Then Rick leaned forward, his hands folded on his legs, and said, "However you got to this point, Marney, we're here to help you find where God wants to take you." He smiled as that sunk in. "It's all about a relationship, much like a dance. Jesus leads, and we follow in a beautiful give-and-take partnership that takes us into His perfect plan for each one of us, individually and as a spiritual family. You are special and unique, and the Lord knows everything about you, including your future."

I said that sounded nice. Then Rick asked if I knew what it was to be saved. I said I did. But I really didn't. Because I wasn't.

They obviously saw right through that and I felt exposed but not judged. Actually, it was kinda nice that they could look past my veneer and care enough to search me out. Donna got up from the couch, knelt in front of me, and softly asked, "Marney, would you like to receive Jesus Christ as your Lord and savior now?"

Her eyes melted into mine. She was so sincere. I nodded and whispered "yes," almost ready to cry. I was weary of the trying. I knew it was time to just dive in.

Rick stood up, reached his hands out to both of us, and I leaned in between them. He looked into my eyes, saying, "The Lord reveals in His Word that now is the day of salvation. He has brought you through all the things that have happened in your life so far, and Donna and I don't need to know the details. But Jesus knows. He's never stopped loving you, and He's been with you all along, hasn't He?"

I nodded, looking him in the eye as tears continued to form. In a flash, I reviewed my life so far. Was it Jesus Who suggested I think of Him when I was attempting transcendental meditation? I remembered how Jesus said He loved me as I left the abortion clinic. Was it actually Jesus who bid the bees to part so I could get a drink in the desert? Maybe it was the living God, creator of heaven and earth, and not a cactus, saying I had much to learn. The urgent desire to become like a virgin, was that the Lord coaxing me? Was it Jesus or a guardian angel warning me to get away fast from Nimai after he socked me? Didn't God tell me He created me to be joyful? And what about Sheila? Hadn't she been a constant, heavenly gift?

I knew in my knower that it had been Jesus sweetly entreating me to recognize His presence and receive His help all along.

"It's really simple," Rick continued. "Just repeat after me and mean it from your heart of hearts. Say this, Marney. Dear Lord Jesus."

He paused, and I whispered, "Dear Lord Jesus."

"I know I need saving." I continued to repeat each phrase after him, my voice gaining volume.

"I can't make myself clean. But You can. You took the punishment I deserved because I sinned against Father God. You died and rose again so that I can be brought by Your righteousness into the family of God. I choose to receive your salvation and forgiveness. I make You the Lord of my life. I am a new creation in You. Thank You, dear Lord. From now on I live to know You and love You and serve You. I know no other gods but You. Amen."

As I repeated each line after him, I felt something lifting off me. It was like I'd been carrying a heavy load and it floated away. My heart filled with sweet warmth that traveled throughout my body. And when the pastor added that last part about not having any other gods, I felt truly free.

I opened my eyes and looked into his. Pastor Rick was beaming. Donna was tearing up. She swept me into her arms and rocked me as we both wept. Rick started worshiping, his hands high, as he rocked back and forth, singing, "Praise God from Whom all blessings flow." We laughed. I signed up for a small Bible study group at the outer office and went into the empty sanctuary. Behind the stage and to the side hung a big cross of coarse dark wood. I knelt at the platform and thanked Jesus for His sacrifice on my behalf. I prayed that He would help me follow Him from then on. Little shivers of joy fluttered in my body.

When I got home, Sheila was sitting out on the patio. She took one look at me and set her book down. She knew. Enveloping me in a hug, this dear friend joyfully exclaimed, "Praise God! Praise You, Jesus!"

If ever there was a day for laughing and crying happy tears, boy, this was it!

Chapter 10

Philippians 3:13, 14 (NIV)

"Brothers and sisters, I do not consider myself yet to
have taken hold of it. But one thing I do: Forgetting
what is behind and straining toward what is ahead, I
press on toward the goal to win the prize for which
God has called me heavenward in Christ Jesus."

THE MORE I LEARNED ABOUT THE BIBLE,
even the Old Testament part I couldn't understand before, the more
I trusted God to be good and powerful enough to accomplish His
goodness. What a relief that I didn't have to be God! When I read
in Isaiah that God's thoughts and ways are higher than ours, just as
the heavens are higher than the earth, I felt so happy. It was liberating.
I was over having to strive to be something I'm not.

Putting it in perspective like this didn't make me feel inferior.
I felt loved, protected, and cherished. That's because the creator
of Heaven and earth cared enough about me to put it all down
in writing. He literally reveals Himself to us through His Word.
Amazing. And so much better than trusting other people to manufacture
some spiritual "knowledge" and then teach me what they
don't know.

There was one little problem, however. As it turns out, I get
scared sometimes. Fear is a big bad meanie. It cripples. Just when I

thought I'd enough faith to steadily progress, something happened that threw me off center. But only for a moment.

I ran into Stuart on campus.

I'd decided to give higher learning another go. I didn't intend to be a caregiver all my life, so I paid for a couple of classes to get my AA finished. I was doing well and aiming to be a nurse, just as Sheila had suggested long before.

As I was leaving the library, I saw Stuart manning a TM table out in the courtyard. A sign announced, "Meditate Your Way to Truth and Peace." Planted in my tracks, I observed him pouring on the charm as he and another man worked to convince a girl to sign up for their class. Stuart was professionally dressed and appeared prosperous. He glanced up and saw me.

At first, he looked startled, and I was about to walk on by without saying a thing. I didn't want a confrontation. A painter's pallet of emotions gripped me: red for anger, yellow for fear, green for envy, and black for regret. But something pulled on me to speak up. I resisted for only a few seconds. Fear faded as resolve entered.

"It's a scam," I said. "They don't have the truth and just want your money."

That got the girl's attention. It also got Stuart's.

"Don't listen to her," he clipped. "She never could discipline herself to follow the simple and proven practice we offer."

"And you never had the discipline or decency to even say goodbye when you left me high and dry!" I shot back and immediately knew it was not a Christian response. I was sweating and trembling.

Now, the girl looked uncomfortable. Stuart was furious. I was interrupting his sale. He struck back with, "You're just a sore loser." He smirked. He thought he had me.

I felt a peaceful presence beside me. I turned my head, but no one was there. No one visible, that is. I was reminded that God loves everybody, even Stuart.

"You're half-right, Stuart," I replied. "I was a loser, and a sore one at that. But since then, I've found freedom in God's love. I've learned I'm not God and neither are you. Meditating all day long won't change that. But the God Who created us and everything else loves us and wants us to know Him personally so He can bless us. He also wants us to love one another. We can't manufacture truth. When we try to find the truth by our own effort without acknowledging the Lordship of God's Son, Jesus Christ, we're just wasting our lives and hurting those we care about."

The only way that could've come out of my mouth was by the Holy Spirit, Who filled and sealed me when I accepted Jesus as my savior. I held my breath, waiting for the explosion.

Stuart's eyes popped, and he burst out laughing. "You're a Christian now? Ha! Ha! *Ha!*

You know, there's something about the name of Jesus Christ. You can talk about God, and people may argue and dance around the subject. But when you mention Jesus, they either soften or go totally ballistic, which is what Stuart did. As Stuart mocked, I told fear to flee. Fast.

While my ex foamed at the mouth, the girl frowned at him and finally piped up, "I don't think that's very funny." She looked at me. "Was he your boyfriend?"

I said that he was. Then, divine inspiration beaned my brain, and I said something that surprised me. Turning to Stuart, I simply said, "I forgive you."

Stuart sputtered, "*You* forgive *me?*"

Now, at this point, a small crowd had gathered. I reached into my book bag and handed the girl a tract that our church prints and advised, "If you want truth, Jesus said 'I am the way, the truth and the life.' He's also the Prince of Peace. He loves you, and He desperately wants to help you have a full and wonderful life. Please give Him a try, first. His grace and mercy are free."

Someone at the back of the gathering clapped. I looked over my shoulder and saw a tall, bearded guy applauding my little speech. He flashed a smile and nodded. I flushed and dipped my eyes, turned to the girl, said, "Jesus bless you," and hurried off to my next class. That's sort of how I first met Casey.

Finishing my homework on Sheila's computer that evening got interrupted when she called and said she'd be late. Paul wanted to see her after work. I sent my assignment off into cyberspace, fixed a smoothie for dinner, and sat out on the patio, reviewing my encounter on campus. My mind lingered on the tall guy with the beard standing behind a few other students. I caught myself fantasizing about him—not in a nasty way, just wondering what he really thought about my spiel. He did clap. And smile. I thought it would be nice to know a man like Paul, a Christian and a real gentleman.

After a few months of living with Sheila, I began to confess to her my gratitude at being saved from all the sin I'd committed—in detail. She never appeared shocked at my admissions nor condemned me. She always ended the conversation every time I spilled the beans about my sordid past by saying, "We all sin, Marney. It's just that some people's problems are more obvious than others. At some point, you really need to let the past go. Don't beat yourself up. You're free now."

I found it hard to accept Sheila as a sinner. She said that everyone since Eve and Adam's fall has been born into a sin consciousness. For some it's false pride. For some it's self-pity. For some it's being a phony. For everyone, it's some form of selfishness.

"Sin," she explained, "is simply being separated from God. That's why we need Jesus. He made a way for us to be with God. He cleanses us by willingly being sacrificed in our place. God is just and holy and will not allow sin into Heaven. Sin leads to death. That's what Hell is, it's eternal separation from God. God would not be righteous and just if He let wrong go unpunished. Jesus took our punishment so we don't have to go to Hell. All we have to do is receive Him as our Lord and savior. Then the Father doesn't see our sin, He just sees Jesus's righteousness when He looks at us.

"Imagine it, Marney. God sent His son, to save us by suffering in our place! That's how much He loves us. We're saved by grace through faith. All we have to do is believe in Jesus. We're Heaven bound, Marney. Isn't it wonderful?"

Although Sheila and I had been friends for a long time, she talked more in our little home together than all the years combined. That's because she loved sharing Jesus. I think it delighted her to finally be able to tell me all the things about Him she had bottled up when I was lost. I couldn't really receive anything from her before. But now, I drank up whatever she poured into me. I just can't express to you how much I grew to love her for that.

Thinking about all this had me tearing up. After all the effort I expended on endeavoring to be good enough at the temple, it was never enough. No matter how many rounds I chanted, or how well I strung flowers on a garland, or tried to follow those regulative principles, I still had no guarantee of salvation, freedom from karma, or assurance of my eternal destination. I simply couldn't save myself no matter what. I needed Jesus's love, just as He first showed me way back when I cried out after leaving the abortion clinic.

Then I remembered that I'd lost my temper at Stuart today. It was going to take a lot of yielding to Jesus's gentle spirit to get to be more like Him. But I'd plenty of help in learning how to continue to live right. I now had the direction of His Word, the Bible, and Christian friends like Sheila, Paul, and my pastors. But today it was the always-present guidance of the Holy Spirit that made an ugly encounter beautiful. Obeying His prompting changed the tone when I offered forgiveness to Stuart, even though I think he wronged me. But you know what? It felt amazing!

I was still basking in the sweet afterglow of these realizations when Sheila got home late that evening.

Chapter 11

Proverbs 16:3 (NIV)

"Commit to the Lord whatever you do, and He will establish your plans."

I KNEW SOMETHING MAJOR WAS UP. Sheila glowed. She thrust out her left hand and wiggled her fingers. A little diamond ring flashed.

After the exclamations and hugs, she told me how Paul proposed. He took her out to dinner and then walked her over to his work van. He told her he found something peculiar in a pipe that day. (It was undoubtedly the only time he ever lied to Sheila.) He extended a piece of PVC toward her hand and shook it. Out slid a little black velvet box.

Then, Paul the plumber went down on his knee and told her she was the female fitting his male valve wanted for life. A little corny, but cute. Anyway, we stayed up late that night, as Sheila revealed her dreams for a wedding and marriage. And children. I went to bed, happy for her and kind of hopeful for myself. Everything she described sounded so wonderful.

As she wound down, Sheila took my hand and said, "Marney, dream big for yourself. Whatever your heart desires, God will surely grant it as long as it's in His perfect will for you. That's His promise."

I did dream that night. But it was more of a nightmare.

Work, school, and life moved along rapidly toward the June date. While Sheila and her mom made their wedding plans, I began to think more and more about what family meant to me. My parents were divorced. Dad remarried and moved to Texas. Mom had a string of boyfriends. That sounds weird, to say that about my mother. But that's what it was. A string. Of boyfriends.

My mother is good-looking for an over-40-year-old. She's also an alcoholic. I'm the only child. I wondered why she was the way she was. Now that I'm a Christian, I wanted to reach out to both of them. The Bible says to honor your parents. So even if my mother didn't seem completely honorable to me, I thought that I should do what God says. And besides, who am I to judge, right?

I called Dad first. His wife answered. She sounded surprised but pleased to hear from me. Dad got on the phone with a reserved, "What's up?" Like he expected me to hit him up for money or something.

"Hey, Daddy," I chirped, sounding like a twelve-year-old. I was that young when they divorced. "I just wanted to let you know I'm thinking about you. How're you doing?"

"Fine, Marney," he was brusque. "June and I are about to go out to dinner. You okay?"

"Yeah, really good. I'm back in college and working. I share a condo with Sheila and . . . and I've been going to church."

"Who's Sheila?" he asked.

"You know, my best friend from elementary to high school? She's going to get married."

"Oh, well, tell her congratulations," he clipped. "We gotta go. Reservations, you know. Take care." He hung up.

Silence closed in on me. "Goodbye, Daddy," I said and pressed the end button.

Just because a person becomes a Christian, doesn't mean they can't have a sour funk. I sat staring at the cell phone in my hand, wondering what'd just happened. And then I sobbed until I got the hiccups. I wished I had a father who loved me.

"I do love you," whispered my heart-held speaker.

"Oh, Jesus," I cried out. "I wish you could hold me in your arms right now!"

"I am," came the reply.

Wow. I wrapped my arms around myself and rocked back and forth, crying until I started laughing. No, I wasn't crazy, just relieved. The more I thought about how many times God had responded lovingly to my pain, the better I felt. Until finally, I just had to laugh. I stood up and tilted my head back, my arms above my head, and shouted out to Heaven, "Thank you, Lord!" I twirled around with arms flung out wide and danced for joy.

What if my earth dad didn't know me and care about me? My Heavenly Father sure did! I felt good. I did something positive. By making the call, I obeyed God. So it didn't go well. What did I expect? We hadn't spoken in over two years! And maybe it wasn't finished yet. If God thought that my dad and I needed to get connected again, He could make a way. Relationship is a two-way street. I took the first step. Good for now.

It was then that I recalled the dream I'd had the night Sheila got engaged. I believe it was based on a real memory of my mother and father. They'd been arguing after I'd gone to bed, a child sucking her thumb and imagining Mommy and Daddy being happy. The dream morphed into a shadowed figure coming into my room and pulling up the covers. I screamed. My mom came in and began hitting him.

Why I didn't recall the dream, or memory, until right then, must be because God was trying to show me something this evening. I felt that the intruder was not my father. But I wasn't sure. Suddenly, I burned to know.

I started to dial my mom but put the phone back down. My heart was pounding. How to do this? I prayed, "Dear God, please help me. Lead me. I need you to let me see what I need to see and say what You want me to say. Help me, Lord, to show Your love to my mother. I know You're here. Thank you, Jesus, for guiding me."

Now, you might think, this girl is a glutton for punishment. But I'd just danced before my Lord. Plus, I prayed. I felt pretty strong in His presence. Besides, once I make a decision to do something, I go through with it.

"Marney, izat really you?" Mom sounded slurry.

"Yes, Mom, I've been thinking about you. How are you?" I went for upbeat.

After a brief hesitation, she coughed and spat out, "Mizzerbul! I'm allalone an' *mizzerbul*!" She sniffed, coughed again, and when she came back on, her voice was muffled, like the phone had slipped somewhere besides her mouth.

I didn't know how to respond. I felt so inadequate. I told her to hang in there. I threw out a "Jesus loves you, Mom," and promised to check back before I hit the end call button.

I wanted to do something. Jump in the car and run over there? And accomplish what? I would've asked Sheila, but she was already in bed and had to get up early the next morning. My great mood had completely disappeared.

"Oh, Jesus," I prayed. "Please help me know what to do!"

A Bible verse saying that the joy of the Lord is our strength came to me.

In that very unjoyful moment, I got another download from Heaven. "There is power in My Name."

And then I got it. Even in my inept attempt to connect with my drunken mother, the name of Jesus jumped past my lips. Maybe, somehow, she caught it. His Name is above every name. It's above foolishness, drunkenness, loneliness, anything that can be named! The joy returned, and I told God that I was releasing my mom to Him. "She's all yours, Lord. I'm going to bed."

That night the dream was about candles. Candles floating on water, candles drifting in the air. Candles on flowering trees and bushes. Candles gliding back and forth on a child's swing. Candles everywhere until the light bathed my sleeping consciousness in glowing, warm light. When I woke up, I knew what to do.

First, I went to the grocery store and bought a rotisserie chicken, potato salad, a jug of sweet tea, and a bouquet of sunflowers and daisies. It was past noon when I pounded on Mom's door. After a long time, I heard her shuffling and complaining, "Who the (blankety blank's) there!"

"It's me, Mom," I called out, and then the squeaky hinges gave way to reveal a drawn, grayish face. She attempted to retrieve one strap of her nighty, which had slid down her shoulder as she swayed back into the house. There was no clear counter space to put my packages, so I set them on the dirty stove. I tried not to cringe at the stink of stale cigarette butts and decaying food in the sink.

I dumped something indescribable out of a glass, filled it with water, and set the flowers on the kitchen table.

"Sidown," she instructed. I sat on a pile of magazines and mail, and Mom sat opposite me amid the filth. She reached for a smoke, but the pack was empty. With another cuss word, she pushed once beautiful blond hair out of her face, leaned back, and stared at the table.

"I brought lunch," I said.

No response.

I looked over at the sink and wished I'd brought dish soap. Then inspiration struck again. "It's a beautiful day, Mom, how about we have a picnic?

She glanced up at me in disbelief. But I persuaded her to get a shower, get dressed, and loaded her and the lunch into Sheila's car. We drove to a park at a spring and natural pool. It was a beautiful balmy afternoon in North Central Florida. Children were playing nearby on swing sets, and families splashed in the spring water. The birds were singing. Mom fidgeted without her cigarettes, but I refused to stop at a store on the way. At first, she was angry about it, but soon the food did its restorative work. As she ate, I began to share my testimony.

"So those are some of the times I heard from Jesus," I wrapped it up. Despite her personal drama, my mom really does love me. She mostly listened, sometimes glancing around at the blooming magnolia trees and gardenia bushes, sometimes staring at the bouquet I brought to the table, and sometimes actually focusing on me.

There's just no disputing someone's personal story. Still, Mom was not immediately ready to believe that God could help her as He'd been helping me. But I trusted she was getting something out of it, and that gave me hope.

"I'm just such a big mess," she whined.

"That's good!" I surprised her. "God loves a nice mess. It gives Him something to work with. Once we admit that we're beyond helping ourselves, then we're ready to let the Lord step in and renovate our hearts and heads." I leaned forward and took her slim, trembling hand. "Now is the day of salvation," I quoted, again from somewhere in the Bible. We had good eye contact when I offered to help her begin a new life right then and there.

"Okay," she sighed and shrugged.

I led her in a prayer. She repeated after me pretty much the same words that my pastor prayed with me when I got born again. Mom was squeezing my hand so hard as she shook, but the words that came out of her mouth starting quietly steadily gained strength so that by the time she said, "Amen!" her face was tearfully vibrant. I sure had those Holy Ghost shivers of excitement. We both took a deep breath. And then I continued to pray for Jesus to cleanse her from cravings for alcohol and cigarettes. I prayed for His joy to fill her to overflow. And I commanded evil spirits away from her.

The weight of sin being lifted away rattled my mom. I knew what that was like, being so radically changed. Unfamiliar territory, even when so much better, can be scary, just because it's different. She almost began lamenting again, when I reminded her that she was now a new person in Christ *and* she had the incredible, powerful gift of Holy Spirit residing in her to make sure she was victorious! I told her to fight the good fight of faith. No holding back. It was a battle for her life, and her life was worth the cost. Jesus paid for her with His precious blood.

She got it. With a radiant smile, Mom said, "I want to go to a store and buy some cleaning supplies."

The thrill of being personally transformed like this never leaves you. And the joy of witnessing the spiritual rebirth of someone else is such a great honor that you can barely contain it. I clapped my hands and laughed. Then, Mom began giggling until it turned into a full belly roar of mirth. Wow! What a day! Thank You, Jesus!

Jaw and shoulders set in determination, she didn't even glance at the customer service counter where cigarettes and lottery tickets are sold when we stopped at a store on the way back to her house. Together, we tackled the entire home until it smelled good. Before leaving, I asked if she wanted me to spend the night.

Mom just said, "Go on home, dear. I'll dust off my Bible. I have some reading to do. But next time you come, we need to talk."

I tell you truly, it was a bona fide miracle.

Chapter 12

Isaiah 43:19 (NIV)

"See, I am doing a new thing! Now it springs up; do you not perceive it? I am making a way in the wilderness and streams in the wasteland."

I'LL NEVER FORGET SHEILA'S WEDDING. By most standards, it was simple. Pastor Rick and the pastor from Sheila's parents' church both officiated. It was at a park, under a canopy with lots of pretty lights overhead and candles on every table. Instead of popular music for dancing, would you believe they had us all queue up, men and boys on one side and women and girls on the other, to do a simple line dance set to Jewish praise music. It was such fun, everyone together, learning the steps, messing up and laughing! By the time the second song played, we all had it down pretty well. Good thing, because this one went faster. At the end, Sheila and Paul stepped along together through the middle of the lines, and everyone shook their hands or hugged them. Paul passed by on the ladies' side and Sheila on the guys.' It was beautiful!

Even Sheila's mom had a great time. And she was so nice to me. As the only bridesmaid, I got a lot of attention. Sheila chose a mint green gown for me that complimented my eyes and red hair. She fussed over me, and I fussed over her. Closer than sisters, that's Sheila and me. And guess who caught the bouquet? My mom!

Now, Mom had been doing pretty well at this point. She'd been going to church with me. And I'd moved in with her since Sheila and Paul were buying a house. I suppose you could say I was Mom's accountability partner. But it was more than that. We had that talk she wanted after our little salvation picnic. Remember when I mentioned a dream when a man tried to molest me? Yes, it actually did happen. It was one of her boyfriends, who she kicked out. What a shock and outrageous insult that someone who was supposed to be into her wanted to mess with her little girl! My mind had disguised the shame of it in such a way that it insidiously manifested in my lying and promiscuous behavior when I grew up without a strong, fatherly figure.

Mom and I were becoming close. We spilled out a lot of confession material about both our pasts. There were even some similarities. I told her about my conversation (if you could call it that) with Dad. She said that he'd always been distant with her. He'd spend so much time at work, in her loneliness, Mom began drinking, which made her more depressed and difficult to get along with. I knew what it felt like to be ignored by a husband and was proud of her for owning that. The women's small group we were attending at church also helped us both. Those ladies made us feel loved and accepted. Plus, we were learning more about how to live in the power of God's beautiful presence.

But about that bridal bouquet. This is funny. I mean, it smacked my astonished mother right in the face, as if to say, "So you think you might get married again? Really?"

She shook that thing like it was a snake! Everyone began clapping in unison, like a march, and my mother strode over to me, thrust those flowers out, and said, "You take it, I'm done!"

We all laughed. I have one of the roses pressed into my Bible.

Being at Mom's had its ups and downs. Sometimes, she'd get the blues. But she didn't go for the bottle. Instead, she'd grab me and the Bible. It didn't matter to her that I was studying for exams, or trying to get out the door to class or work. Her need was urgent, and I wanted her to succeed. So I'd humor her and, what do you know? I'd get spiritually fed, as well. And right when I needed it.

She loved the Psalms, especially the 91st. It talks about making God our habitation, a place where we do life with Him constantly. He's our shelter, our deliverer. He covers us with His eagle wings. Would you believe God *honors* us? Just because we know His name and take shelter of Him God gives *us* honor! I think that's pretty amazing, don't you?

I got back into painting. I made Mom a picture of feathers floating down from a brilliant blue sky and enveloping a figure that's supposed to look like her. It made her cry. She hung it over her bed. I know she's struggling, but the Apostle Paul struggled, too. He said to just keep fighting the good fight of faith, to finish the course and not give up, no matter what.

Painting really helps me to process my thoughts. I came across another verse and immediately put it onto canvas. When the prophet Isaiah lamented at all the sin among the people, God comforted and encouraged him with the words, "Arise and shine, for your light has come and the glory of the Lord has risen upon you." Funny, but when I was a little girl, I remember my mom getting me up for school, saying "Rise and shine, Marney." I didn't know that she was sort of quoting the Bible. She probably didn't, either.

Anyway, I splashed big block letters screaming, *"ARISE!"* across a colorful sunrise peaking over an ocean horizon. It's above my bedhead. Great place for it, huh?

Earlier in that chapter of Isaiah, the Lord promised to guide this man continually, and satisfy his soul in the bad times. I wanted that promise, to be "like a watered garden, and like a spring of water, whose waters fail not." Helping Mom helped me. I got more and more into God's Word until I fell in love with it. Here was the transcendental truth and joy I had previously pursued but couldn't find—until I found Jesus.

In addition to my clients at Sheila's old condominium, I took a part-time job at my college's bookstore. My grades were up, and so I got back into a scholarship program. I finally saved up enough money to buy a decent used car, cash. Dad was still supporting Mom with alimony, and I helped out, too. She began volunteering at the church and eventually got hired in their office part time. We were able to get her house painted and a new couch.

One day, I was stocking shelves at the campus bookstore, when I heard a deep male voice rumble at my back, "Hey Red, still sockin' it to the phony yogis?"

It sounded like he was right in my ear, and I startled, dropping books and jumping up, almost plowing backward into the tall, bearded guy who'd clapped when I had the little run in with Stuart.

He put a big hand on my arm to steady me and helped me pick the mess up. Finally catching my breath, I sarcastically retorted that I'd enough demons of my own to fight off, lately. Now, that wasn't entirely sound doctrine and sounded pretty stupid, but he looked deeply into my eyes (he has nice brown eyes) and said that he'd like to hear more about that if I wanted someone to talk to.

I did.

Chapter 13

Proverbs 3:5–6 (NIV)

"Trust in the Lord with all your heart and lean not
on your own understanding; in all your ways submit
to Him, and He will make your paths straight."

SINCE SHEILA GOT MARRIED, I SAW LESS
of her, and I missed our conversations. But she was in a new season
of her life and maybe so was I. Or, at least, I was getting closer to it.
As busy as I was with school, work, church, and Mom, I felt a little
lonely at times. I'd made new friends at church, but there was no
one like my Sheila. Only, she was no longer mine. She was Paul's.

Well, during this period, I learned some patience. Sheila had
advised me to dream big for myself. Is it envy when you want what
your friend has? Not that I wanted Paul, for Heaven's sake. But I
did like the idea of being, well, married—finally, actually belonging
with a man. The right man. But to get there, I realized I had to
be the right woman. So I accepted this time as God's preparation
period for me to be a qualified wife. That meant, I'm sure, to be sol-
idly grounded in my own identity as a daughter of the Most High
God, continuously being sanctified by His Holy Spirit and enriched
with His Word.

When Casey offered to listen if I wanted someone to talk to,
I kinda froze. Yes, of course I wanted someone to talk to. Who
doesn't? But a guy? The only male persons I knew that I could trust

were Christians. And not even all of them because it takes time to get to know someone well enough to expose your heart and mind. By this time, I'd been through enough that I'd rather keep to myself than blab to the wrong person.

After a heartbeat's hesitation, I blew him off. And immediately regretted it. As he was walking toward the door with his package, I hurried over to him and said that if he was serious, we could meet in the food court in an hour. He said he'd be out of class in two hours. I said that'd be okay.

Then, he dropped his voice, "You can trust me, you'll see that I'm no wolf, Little Red Riding Hood." With a wink and a grin, he was gone, and I began counting down the minutes.

Oooh, the man had charm. But was that God's provision for me? My guard was up when I walked over to a booth in the campus food court. He had two protein shakes on the table and stood up as I sat down.

With hand extended, he said, "My name's Casey McKay. Do you prefer strawberry or mango?"

When I said, "Mango," he set one of the big cups in front of me and sat down. We stared at each other a moment. He gestured to the drink. I drank. He drank. We both looked up at the same time. He grinned. And I caught the humor of the situation. A smile snuck out of me, too.

Instead of asking what I was studying or some other normal conversation opener, he just launched into the heart of the matter.

"It's impossible to know who to trust unless God shows us," he began. "Personally, I'm learning to trust the Lord in everything I do or don't do. That's why I'm here with you right now. When you challenged those TM guys, you looked scared. But something fantastic happened there. It's like a light came on. You became confident and spoke the truth about Jesus to them and that girl. So, tell me, what happened to you there?"

"What do you mean?" I was searching my memory.

"How is it that you went from timid to bold and from argumentative to, well, humble and gentle." He laughed. "I don't even know your name, and I'm asking all these questions!"

"Marney, Marney White," I replied. "Uh, well, what happened is that I felt Holy Spirit nudge me. I was later ashamed at the way I acted."

"Why, Marney Marney White," he lightly challenged. "If Holy Spirit came to your aid and guided you and you obeyed Him, you have nothing to be ashamed of. Remember, there's no condemnation for those in Christ."

I considered that and found it to be true. Then, it occurred to me that he'd observed an awful lot that day. "How long were you there to see all this?"

"Oh, I'd been watching those guys awhile. I even talked to them, myself," he answered. "I tried to tell them about Jesus, but they weren't exactly interested. So I just stood by to see what their game was, and then you came along."

Casey leaned back, his drink finished, and he pulled on his beard thoughtfully. I wondered what he'd look like clean shaven. He crossed his arms over his chest, covering an image of a cross on his T-shirt and the words "Follow Me."

"I've only been a Christian a year, now," I admitted. "Do you go to church?"

"Actually, no, but I'd like to," he dropped his chin down and looked up at me from lowered brows. "I have my son on the weekends."

Now, that right there could be an exploratory acquaintanceship killer. However, it sparked my curiosity. "How old is he?" I asked.

Casey, reached for his phone, and flashed a picture of a toddler riding on his shoulders, both of them wearing matching red ball caps that said, "USA."

"Marcus just turned two here," Casey proudly explained. "He's almost three now and awesome!"

Suddenly, I realized that I needed to get over to the condominium to take care of my client. I was going to be late if I didn't hurry, and it was her laundry day. I told Casey that I had to get to another job. I thanked him for the drink.

He sprung up as I stood and asked, "Marney, can I pray with you before you leave?"

Surprised, I said, "Sure."

He reached for my hand, "Dear Lord, thank You for showing Marney Your will for her life and for helping her to completely trust and follow You. Bless her, dear Lord, and protect her as she goes her way. In the name of Jesus. Amen."

"Uh, thanks," I said. "Hey, why don't you and Marcus come to my church? They have a great program for little kids there with a playground and everything."

"Where?" he called as I started toward the door.

"Family Faith Fellowship," I said. "On Martin Luther King Street. Ten o'clock."

What had I done?

Mom was washing dishes when I got home later that evening. "When are you going to call your father?" she asked for the second time.

From our talks, she recognized my need to feel validated by him. That Mom was considering my desire to be reconnected with Daddy demonstrated her newfound sensitivity. Instead of whining and complaining about her own situation, she wanted to see my paternal problem resolved for my peace of mind. It really shook her up when I told her about that nightmare. I had previously asked her if it had anything to do with my own father. I already told you that it had been one of Mom's boyfriends that tried to violate me. Mom assured me that, although Daddy had typically been detached from our family, her ex-husband would never have abused either of us. Of course, neglect can be seen as a kind of abuse, though not as overt. I think of it as the sin of omission. We can sin by doing wrong things. We can also sin by not doing right things. Even so, she wanted me to feel whole when it came to my paternal relationship, despite his standoffishness.

Thinking about meeting Casey and his son at church had pushed most other subjects, like trying to call Daddy again, to the background. I told Mom about our talk on campus. She liked the idea of them coming to our church. She also liked that he prayed for me. So did I, even though I had to keep pushing away worry that maybe I'd been too forward.

As she put the last dish in the drainer, Mom just said that maybe we should get to the church early and dropped the other topic about calling Texas.

Sheila called that night. "Marney, I'm thrilled. Pastor Rick's asked Paul to give the prayer on Sunday!"

Sheila went on to explain that Pastor Rick had been pleased with Paul's dedication to the youth program at Family Faith Fellowship. This Sunday, the youth were going to be participating in the service, and that's why he wanted Paul on the platform to lead the congregation in praying for the teens. I told her that Paul would do an amazing job of it and how happy I was for her that her husband was being appreciated, as he should be. I also told her about Casey and Marcus.

"Oh, Marney," she responded. "I'm so glad you're bringing them. Please sit up front with us so we can all be together."

It took me a half hour of trying on clothes before climbing in bed that night. I needed to go shopping. I wanted to put my best foot forward this Sunday. Come to think of it, I'd need new shoes, too.

Chapter 14

Hebrews 10:24–25 (NIV)

"And let us consider how we may spur one another on toward love and good deeds, not giving up meeting together, as some are in the habit of doing, but encouraging one another—and all the more as you see the Day approaching."

PAUL DID A GREAT JOB OF LEADING THE congregation in prayer as he presented the graduates from Teen Victory on stage. He put his arm around each of the 20 or so kids, naming the boy or girl and getting everyone to specifically pray for that person's gifting. I thought it demonstrated God's unique love for each person and really made me think that I ought to pursue my gifting. I just wasn't entirely sure of what it was.

At first, Marcus protested being left with strangers at Tots' Sunday school. But Casey stayed with him a bit, and when his little boy saw other children playing and laughing, he traipsed over to join in. We exited without another tear. Mom and I had met them in the lobby. I was glad we all got there early so they could get oriented.

Family Faith Fellowship is a nice-size church, not so big that you feel lost in the crowd. But it's big enough to offer plenty of programs to help members get to know the Lord and one another. FFF also sponsors a variety of local ministries. Since Mom was now working in the church office, she'd tell me about how our offerings were used to support underprivileged people in the area. She'd even started donating her time as a church affiliated mentor at the local rehab center. Helping other people like that turned on her power switch. It brought Mom so much energy and joy. She was truly blossoming.

I sat between Casey and Sheila on the front row. Mom sat on Casey's other side. During the sermon, Pastor Rick told us to tap the person next to us and say, "You were made for more!" He'd been teaching out of the book of Ephesians where the Apostle Paul was telling the early Church to open the eyes of their understanding so they could know what is the hope of God's calling on their lives. He spoke about the glory of the Lord's riches, His blessings, for those who believe in Jesus. Receiving these blessings brings out of us God's power to do His wonderful work. Again, I thought of Mom and how this truth applied to her abounding life.

Well, Mom gave Casey a flat-handed slap on the back and shouted, "You were made for more, Casey!" Rick heard her amid all the other voices and looked straight at my new friend. He called him up to the platform.

With a slightly baffled look, Casey stepped up and over to my pastor's podium. Rick put his hand on Casey's shoulder and pronounced, "Son, God has shown me that you know Him, but you're allowing many cares to keep you at a distance. Do you want to break free from these limitations?"

Casey visibly swallowed hard (bobbing that beard), looked the man straight on, and said, "Yes, sir, I sure do."

Rick then prayed softly. I strained to hear, but the organist began playing in the background. Maybe it was supposed to be a private moment, just between a young man, a man of God, and the Lord. When Casey turned around to exit the stage, he gave me a wobbly grin.

Seated, he said, "Thanks, Red."

Sheila squeezed my hand and nodded, sniffing. Paul, now sitting on the other side of Sheila, reached over to Casey and shook his hand.

Mom just poked him and said, "Told ya!"

Sometimes the order of the service would shift. Usually, the worship singing was all at the beginning. This time, Pastor Rick called the worship team back to the stage after he was done teaching on the urgent need for the Church, the body of Christ, to be of one accord.

"You have one physical body, but it has many parts," he preached from the Book of First Corinthians. "All its many parts have unique functions, and they all work together for the good of the whole. It's the same with Christ. We were all baptized by one Holy Spirit. And so we're formed into one spiritual body. Don't ever think that you can properly operate separate from His body. We need one another to be complete, fitly joined to work together for the Lord. That's the joy of fellowship. You're never alone. We not only have the Holy Spirit to lead and guide us individually, we have each other. We're on the same team, and we have the same leader, Jesus, the head of the body we're a part of."

So when he called the singers and musicians back, they launched into, "One goal, one vision to see You exalted. We are the body of Christ." Standing next to me, Casey caught the spirit of the song as he followed the words appearing on the screen. He let his baritone soar and raised his hands. The vibration of his singing resonated in my breast, and I got the shivers. I felt like flying. Sheila and Paul started swaying right and left to the beat. Mom joined in. The whole front row picked it up and, like waves, the motion caught on throughout the big room. It was a beautiful flowing of peace and joy. The whole body, moving together, simply relishing the truth of the Lord's presence connecting us in His beautiful, powerful love.

After collecting Marcus, who didn't want to leave, Mom, Casey, and I walked out to the parking lot with plans to go over to Sheila and Paul's house for lunch. My car wouldn't start. It just went click click click when I turned the key. Mom said it sounded like the battery. I lifted the hood. Fortunately, the person next to me was pulling out. Leaving Marcus with us, Casey parked his truck in that spot and lifted his hood. Soon, he had the cables connected.

But even after a while of trying to jump it, my car kept quiet, not even clicking.

Out came Sheila and Paul, leaving the church after us because they'd been talking with Teen Victory parents. After a short powwow during which Casey and Sheila exchanged numbers, Mom and Marcus, along with his booster seat, transferred to their car. I got into Casey's truck to go to Walmart to get a new battery.

As he hoisted my old battery onto his truck bed, Sheila winked and said, "It sure is nice to have a man who knows how to fix things!" Whoo boy! That made me flush, 'cause Casey heard her. He just replied in that deep, determined voice, "It's not fixed yet, but it will be."

If you want to know what someone is like, just go Walmarting with them. Know what I mean? I get distracted easily. I stopped at a display of flower bouquets. As I pondered which one to pick, Casey pulled on his beard. He was a man on a mission. He offered to meet me at the checkout as he began pushing the cart past me to the automotive department. I quickly grabbed a colorful mix of blossoms and skipped after him. No way was I going to lose him in that big place! Besides, I realized he might be anxious to get to his son, who he'd just left with new acquaintances.

A little over an hour later, we rolled into Sheila and Paul's driveway. Casey followed me there after getting my car started. He'd already talked to his son. Sheila called Casey to let him know that Marcus was enjoying a bowl of Jell-O and watching a cartoon. Somehow, Sheila had managed to serve the happy child his favorite flavor.

"Orange, Daddy!" Marcus spit into the short conversation and handed the phone back to my charmed friend. *Dora the Explorer* had come back on.

With his long bed beside my little car (which fired up immediately with its new battery), Casey and I walked up to the open side door and were greeted by Paul. He snagged Casey by handing him a tray of hamburgers, and together they went to the backyard to cook. Mom was chopping salad ingredients and put me to work hunting condiments.

Sheila came into the kitchen from the family room with an empty bowl. "I hope he has room for lunch," she said. "He just devoured two servings of Jell-O!" She saw the splash of colorful flowers already in a vase. "Ah, Marney, my favorites."

Finally, with everything assembled, we settled around the dining table and held hands to pray. Paul not only blessed the food in Jesus's name, he blessed each of us in his down-home way.

"We're fixin' to eat this great food, Lord," he said. "Just keep us eating Your words as we enjoy burgers and one another. And thanks, God, we love Ya!"

Marcus only ate half of his burger. Wiping his orange mustache, he asked Sheila for more Jell-O, which Casey okayed. After clearing the table, we all joined Marcus in the family room to watch an episode of *Super Book*, a cartoon series about Bible heroes. When Casey asked how they happened to have a children's DVD, Paul looked over at Sheila, who nodded.

He cleared his throat and announced, "We'll be needin' it for our own kid."

Now, I already knew that Sheila was expecting. In fact, I was with her when she took her first pregnancy test. Since then, I'd been buying up little items. Baby shopping is the most fun! One day, when Mom was watching Christian TV, we saw the promo for these colorful, instructive Bible cartoons; I knew I had to get them. And maybe, someday, I can borrow them back for, you know, my own kid. Some day.

While Marcus was enthralled with the excitement of learning about Noah and his family building the arc before the impending flood, we adults got to know more about Casey.

Paul started out with, "Hey man, you've got a great kid. I'm learning by watchin' you." He lowered his voice. "What's the deal with the momma?"

Casey looked at each of us and settled on me. "We were going to get married straight out of high school. She cheated on me. I was pretty upset and quit going to church. I tried to win her back. We got pregnant." He flourished his hand at Marcus, as if to say, "Ta da!"

I was feeling a little uncomfortable, the way he kept looking at me. Casey has intensely dark eyes, almost black. Piercingly, that's how he watched my reaction. But I kept cool because I really cared about his story.

"She still didn't want to marry me," he continued. "She's dating another guy now. I'm not thrilled. But at least she's a decent mother, and that's all I can hope for at this point. Eventually, whenever I get married, I'd like to try and get full custody."

Sheila piped up. "Marriage is so good with the right person. You're blessed that you found out about her infidelity beforehand. God's got the right woman for you and your sweet little boy." She turned to Paul. "Pray for him, honey."

Paul smiled and nodded at Casey. "Sure, baby. Dear Lord, Your timin' is always perfect. You know what it takes to put a family together, 'cause you invented family along with everything else. So take charge of the plan, Sir. Prepare Casey and his future wife for the long haul of life. No leaks, no breaks. Just that flow of living water by Your Holy Ghost, leadin' and guidin' them both into Your perfect will. For Your glory, Jesus. Amen."

After the group "Amen," Mom reminded our new friend, this time more gently, "You really were made for more, son." She looked at me. "We all were."

Casey and I simultaneously murmured, "Amen." He wagged thick, black eyebrows at me and chuckled.

That night, I sat with Mom, talking about what had happened. She scooched next to me on the couch and took my hand. "Marney, dear, you need to quit worrying about your past." How did she read my mind? "Just let the Lord take care of it. Remember what we learned in Bible class? His grace is sufficient. Just be at peace in His care and let the past go. We're new creations in Christ, okay? Old things have passed away."

"Okay, Mom," I whispered. I was really liking Casey. A lot. But the last thing I needed to do was rush into something. While walking back out to the cars to leave Sheila and Paul's, he asked me for a date. We decided on dinner the next Friday. We'd only just met, really. But I guess it was okay for us to see more of each other. What harm could that do, right?

Before going to bed, I called Sheila. "What do you think?" I asked as soon as she answered.

"Oh, He's for real," she responded. "Paul and I could tell immediately. What you need to do is quit worrying about your past and just let things develop according to God's grace. Did he ask you out for a date? I saw you talking out in the driveway."

Sheila and I wrapped it up with her praying for me, and then I went into the bathroom to brush my teeth. Looking intensely in the mirror, I spoke to my soul to be quiet and let God be God. And the new me be me. Taped to the top of the mirror was a note saying, "My peace I give to you." I slept really well that night.

Chapter 15

James 3:17–18 (NIV)

"But the wisdom that comes from heaven is first of all pure; then peace-loving, considerate, submissive, full of mercy and good fruit, impartial and sincere. Peacemakers who sow in peace reap a harvest of righteousness."

ALL THAT WEEK I WRESTLED WITH MY mind. There was a lot I was unsure about. I didn't know if I really wanted to go into nursing. At first, I thought it would be a good thing because it pays well and you help people. But the more I thought about it, the more I doubted. Science is not my forte. I didn't care for biology in high school. Sure, I still wanted to help people, but how best to do that? Now that my associate of arts degree was wrapping up, I needed to fine-tune my plan and not waste that scholarship money or my time.

Friday rolled around, and the date with Casey loomed over me with excitement and dread. Did I have what it takes to be the kind of woman who could love him and his son? What did I know about little boys? For that matter, what did I know about having a healthy, well-balanced, and God-honoring relationship with a man?

That afternoon, I decided to invoke further abuse on my psyche. I called my dad again.

This time, he answered. "Hey, Marney." Did he sound a bit contrite? "I'm sorry I had to cut you off before. I guess you might have thought I was rude."

"Uh, well, I guess I called at a bad time," I excused him. "Is this an okay time, now?"

He chuckled nervously. "Yeah. Well, June thought I sounded rude to you. So, anyway, uh, so . . . you're in school, huh?"

I said I was but was unsure of what direction to go in. Dad reminded me that there was always opportunity in business. Of course, he'd push that because he's a successful businessman. We talked for about ten minutes and caught up a bit. He was happy to hear that Mom had quit drinking and was doing so well. He didn't invite me to visit him or anything like that. But all in all, it was a milestone conversation.

As I threw outfits on the bed, desperately trying to decide what to wear that night, I managed to thank the Lord for Dad and I reconnecting. By the time Casey rang the doorbell, I was assembled in skinny jeans and a blousy, seashell-patterned smock top with three-inch wedge sandals, and dangly earrings shaped like dolphins. I put my hair back in a wavy fall and called me done.

Casey whistled and got up from a living room chair when I walked in. Mom said I looked nice and nautical. I thought he looked amazing in a crisp white shirt, new jeans, and black boots. Best of all, he'd trimmed that bush on his face and gotten a haircut. Uh, huh!

Riding in his truck felt familiar and close, even with the big console between us. With his arm flung over the seat back, he gave my shoulder a little squeeze and asked if the local steak house would suit me. Believe me, after being a vegetarian, it more than appealed.

We settled into a back booth with a lantern on the table giving a warm glow to his dark eyes. I really wanted to know more about Casey, and he obliged. He said that his passion was cars. That would explain the holes and grease splotches in his T-shirts since he'd been taking welding classes and learning everything automotive.

"What I really want to do is custom body work," he explained. He showed me some pictures on his phone of a restoration he and his dad did on a 1972 Oldsmobile Cutlass.

"My dad worked all his life at body shops, and I'd hang out there whenever I could since I was a kid," he said with enthusiasm. "But I wanted to learn more about running a shop. I think I can expand on what I know about automotive paint and body and have my own business someday."

I asked where the car was now. He said he really didn't know. His father had passed away before Marcus was born. "Last I knew, Mom still had it the garage, but she was thinking of selling it," he sighed. "I guess she needs the money, and I sure can't afford to buy it."

It wasn't terribly late when he got me home. He had to work in the morning. Casey has two jobs, as well as going to college. During the week he works at a car parts store. Saturday mornings he works at a lumber yard and then picks Marcus up in the afternoon and has him through Sunday night.

He didn't kiss me good night. He cocked his head, leaned in, and started to, then changed his mind. We hugged. I went to bed happily looking forward to seeing him and Marcus at church Sunday. But I kind of wished he'd kissed me.

My mom had become a fanatic. So off to church we rushed to arrive early. Again. She loved to stand in the lobby and greet people. I sat down by the door and waited. Before long, in came Casey and Marcus, who was pulling on his daddy's hand and waddling as fast as his little legs could take him to Sunday school. Casey just winked and let the little guy drag him off. Was that beard shorter?

Yep. As we finally settled in our chairs in the sanctuary, I took a good look. A definite jaw outline had appeared. He turned to me, stroked a shorn cheek, and grinned. I blushed but smiled back.

"So, Red, have you heard from God about what to do with school?" he asked. We'd discussed my impending decision over our rib eyes Friday night. I told him that I'd seen an advisement counselor but was still uncertain. He suggested that I pray about it. I had.

"Nope, no answer yet," I replied.

Butting in, Mom said, "Better take care of business, Marney." She'd borrowed my skinny jeans, and I think she looked way too good in them. Hoo boy! Was I jealous of my mother, now?

Just as I was checking my attitude, the worship team erupted in "Love One Another," by Michael J. Smith. This morphed into Casting Crowns' rendition of "Joyful Joyful We Adore You."

Mom turned to me with teary eyes and mouthed, "I love you."

Pastor Rick bounded onto the stage and cried into the mic, "Lord, teach us to love each other! The world will know us as Yours by how we do!" The singing continued, and I felt a true epiphany. So what if my mom looked great in tight jeans? She was living like a woman devoted to Jesus Christ. So what if I was at a crossroads in my education? God had a plan, and I'd better quit comparing myself to other people, like Sheila, and tune in to His direction for me. And so what if the man standing next to me singing his heart out looked like a rodeo star? If God wanted us together for life, He'd make a way.

I shouted out: "I trust you, Jesus! Take over! I'm all yours!"

"Yeah!" Casey hollered and gave me a one-armed hug.

Mom hooked her arm in mine and swayed. Again, we rocked together, the three of us. And what do you know? The whole row rocked. Then the section rocked and reeled, and soon everyone was doing the dance of love and unity as the worship team got louder. It's sort of become a thing in this church. I get shivers every time I think back on it.

"I love this church," Casey commented afterward as he sat at our kitchen table.

"Me, too, Daddy," Marcus mumbled around a mouth full of PB and J. "Grape, yum."

"And you have the purple mustache to prove it," Mom wiped the new favorite flavor off his chin.

We adults were enjoying turkey sandwiches and coleslaw when Mom's phone rang. She got up to converse with a lady from church about plans for a fellowship dinner next week. I took our dishes to be rinsed and felt a warmth looming behind me. Casey reached around me to deposit Marcus's cup in the sink, brushing my arm. Penetrating black eyes held mine for just a moment. He turned back to collect his son, explaining that he needed to get him to his mother soon. I sighed. I hated to see them go. I hugged Marcus. Mom came back in to say goodbye. Casey gave me a resigned hand wave. They left. I sighed again.

Mom felt for me. "Sweetie, you're falling in love. Don't let it scare you. Just go slow and keep reaching for the Lord's strong hand to guide you through. I'm convinced that, if you stay strong in your conviction to be pure, Father God will grant your heart's desire."

To emphasize the message, God had Sheila call me that night. As busy as she was, preparing a nursery, still working full time, and helping her husband with his business and ministry, dear wonderful Sheila had me on her heart.

"Marney," she began, "Paul and I want to get together with you and Casey next week. When might be a good time?"

We worked out a rough idea for next Friday night at their house. I called Casey, and he swiftly accepted. After calling Sheila back to confirm, I asked what I could bring. She just said, "Bring that Bible I gave you."

Now, about my Bible. I told you before how much I'd grown to love it. Currently in the Book of Isaiah, I was enchanted by the 40th chapter. Remember how I'd not liked the Old Testament way back when I was following my heathen ways? Well, let me tell you, there are some precious treasures there if you dig. In this chapter, the Lord encourages his prophet who had been tasked with warning the Jewish people about idolatry and God's judgment.

The Lord tells Isaiah that He'll be sending another great man of God to warn the people to repent and prepare to receive Lord Jesus. This is a famous prophecy about John the Baptist hundreds of years before Christ came. Then, God challenges the reader to name anyone who could be greater than Himself. "Who has directed the Spirit of the Lord, or being His counselor has taught Him? (v. 13) "Lift up your eyes on high and behold Who has created these things, that brings out their host by number: He calls them all by names by the greatness of His might, for He is strong in power; not one falls" (v. 26).

In verse 29, the Lord says that He gives power to the weak and concludes with one of my favorites in verse 31. "But they that wait upon the Lord shall renew their strength, they shall mount up with wings of eagles; they shall run and not be weary; and they shall walk and not faint."

All that week, as I went about my daily life, I reflected on this idea of mounting up on eagle wings. I read about eagles on the Internet. They love storms. That's when they get to soar. The other birds cower down below when things get rough. But not eagles. They catch the updraft and just sail above the clouds. Isn't that magnificent?

Thinking about waiting upon the Lord gave me hope and courage. So when I met with my friends that Friday night, I was at ease and eager to see what Sheila had in mind for this get together. Sitting in their living room, snacks on the coffee table, Paul started us off with a request for a song. I asked if he knew one about waiting on the Lord. He picked up his guitar, strummed for some chords, and sang slowly a Hillsong United number, "Here I am waiting abide in me I pray . . . Come live in me . . . and I will rise on eagles' wings."

Like a lullaby of comfort and an anthem of trust, we sang and sang these beautiful words until we hushed and just sat quietly, resting in the glow of God's sweet presence. Eventually, we came back to one another, exchanging smiles and comments like, "Thank you, Jesus" and "Praise You, Lord."

Chapter 16

Colossians 4:6 (NIV)

"Let your conversation be always full of grace, seasoned with salt, so that you may know how to answer everyone."

OUR GET-TOGETHERS AT SHEILA AND Paul's house became a monthly event. That first visit was so satisfying, and it was a great way for Casey and me to learn about each other without rushing into a scenario that could easily trip us up with too much physical contact. We'd frankly discussed how we didn't want our relationship to become tainted. There was definite heat between us. Admitting attraction to lust is one thing. Acting on it is another. As Christians, we knew we had to walk that fine line of obedience, no matter how our bodies felt. Familiarly seeking the Lord together like this put our relationship on a higher platform. If it were not for that, I have no doubt we would've already been in the sack, undermining our reverence for God's leading in this relationship, as well as respect for one another's integrity. We were becoming a couple without coupling, you get it?

At the same time, I'd decided what to do about school. While waiting at a dentist's office a few days after our first Friday night gathering, the piped-in classic rock song "Taking Care of Business" came on. That did it. How many times did I need to hear this? First Dad, then Mom, and now this wonky old song. Plus, I didn't tell you that the sermon on Sunday had been titled "Doing God-Business." Pastor preached about the necessity for Christians to have good Biblical ethics and standards in how we conduct ourselves in every aspect of our lives, particularly in handling money. He explained that there was nothing wrong with money as long as we didn't love it. People can make an idol of their wealth or lack of it, you see. I prayed that night and got a real peace about my decision. That song simply confirmed it right before the receptionist called me back to get my teeth cleaned.

Extra bonus, I was now enrolled in some of the same classes as Casey. We were both headed for a BAS in organizational management.

One Saturday, Casey asked me to take care of Marcus. The lumber yard was receiving a big shipment and was short of help, so he was called to extra duty. I arrived at his place at 7:00 a.m., and we loaded a sleepy little boy into my car, along with a cache of toys and other kiddy paraphernalia. I'd been to his apartment before to study with another student. Talk about Spartan living. Plain, plain, *plain*. But neat and clean, just like his truck.

Anyway, as I unhooked Marcus from his car seat at Mom's, he gave a big yawn, reached up his little arms, and hugged my neck. He smelled good. With his head nestled against my chest, I fell in love. Suddenly, I was all about this little guy. I really wanted to know him. That day, I learned what it feels like to be a mother. My worldview shifted to revolve around another one, so dependent, innocent, and trusting. We played and ate Jell-O. It was wonderful! I hated to see him go when Casey collected him that evening.

As God settled my life into a routine that now outlined a clear manifesto in my mind, I began to glimpse possibilities I'd previously only fantasized about. Marriage beckoned. Casey had Marcus at Christmas because his ex was on a cruise to the Bahamas with her latest boyfriend. We spent it together at Mom's. Now two and a half, our adorable little boy plunged into his packages with the gusto of joy to rip, shred, and tear into things especially meant for him. As Marcus exulted over toys and I took pictures, Casey slipped something onto my lap. No little box, no gimmick. Just a pink diamond ring set in deep gold. As the *brumm brumm* imitation engine sound of a plastic truck trundled by under kid power, Casey knelt in front of me and simply said, "Marry me, Red."

Not exactly romantic, I know. He didn't say he loved me. Maybe it's because he works with metal a lot that Casey seems a little hard. But his eyes said it. I caught my breath and forgot to speak. He took my hand in his rough one and gently slid the ring on. Perfect fit. Done deal.

Mom clapped. Marcus looked up from maneuvering the truck between her legs at the foot of the couch. The world stood still. I slipped off the chair and into Casey's arms on the floor. With my face buried in his plaid flannel shirt, I just whispered "I love you."

"Me too, Marney," he breathed into my hair. "Me too."

"Me too, Daddy!" out popped Marcus.

"Me three," Mom echoed. "Or would it be four?"

We all laughed.

Soon after that, it happened again on campus. I ran into an old acquaintance. Or, you might say, ex "husband." Nimai and I were never legally married, but we did live together as husband and wife for a brief time. To make things more intense, I was with Casey when it happened.

As soon as I heard the rhythmic *"ching ching ching"* ringing of hand cymbals, I knew what we'd encounter around the corner outside the student union. We'd just finished midterms, and both did well. Studying together with one's fiancé under the umbrella of mutually agreed upon celibacy can be quite productive. We were highly motivated to spur each other onto success. We had ideas for our own family business and were eager to move into the plans we knew God had for us.

Anyway, Casey stopped to observe the chanting party. I hooked my arm in his and gave a tug. Try moving 220 pounds and over six feet of muscle when you only weigh 125. The look he gave me asked, "What?"

Up to now we'd left a lot of my past where it belonged—in the trash can. (Read: undisclosed.)

With a ring on my finger, I should've felt somewhat confident. But Casey, extra humanly sensitive to color, no doubt because he loves painting cars in unlimitedly subtle shades that only an expert can distinguish, noticed my reddening face. When I blush, it creeps down my neck and mottles the top of my chest. It's awful. I looked like an exploded freckle.

He walked me over to the empty picnic table under the widespread arms of a live oak. "Why is that guy staring farts at us?" he wondered.

I quoted from the fifth chapter of the book of James. "Therefore, confess your sins to each other and pray for each other so that you may be healed. The prayer of a righteous person is powerful and effective."

Memorizing Bible verses is probably the smartest thing I've ever done, besides accepting the salvation of Jesus Christ. Casey let the verse sink in and listened with remarkable receptivity as I told him about my foray into the Krishna society and disastrous arranged marriage with the guy singing the mantra very loudly over on the plaza.

"Marney," Casey soothed, "you don't have to apologize to me for any mistake in your past. I'm just glad you don't have any more ties to it." He paused to collect himself and continued. "I trust you. Is there any other one that might pop up?" He chuckled. "First the TM boyfriend and now this guy in an orange sheet!" He became serious. "You can trust me, you know?"

I said that I trusted him completely and I'd tell him anything he wanted to know about me. He just said, "Let's pray."

So, we held hands on the cement tabletop and bowed our heads in the shade of that ancient tree. This is why I know that Casey and I are right for each other. We've learned to give it up to the Lord, no matter what the doubt or trouble. This was early on in our long journey, but it was already a pattern for doing life together.

"Dear Father," Casey said. "Thank You for bringing Marney and I into Your family. Lord, You know that Marney was intending to find you when she got sidelined into that cult, and You know all about whatever else she tripped out on along her way to Your truth. I just thank you, Lord, that you brought Marney and I together. Bless us, Father God, to grow closer to You as we grow closer together. Help us to know You and know one another as You created us to be in Your divine likeness. We humbly ask You to abundantly bear Your fruit through our union in Jesus's holy name. Amen."

I squeezed his hands as I echoed the amen and wiped the damp on my cheek. "Thank you, Casey," I sniffed.

"No, thank *you*," he returned. "Before I met you and got back in fellowship, I was missing out on a lot, just worrying about how to make ends meet and ignoring God. Since we've both been working and tithing God's portion at church, we're actually getting somewhere." Thinking about the future gets Casey excited.

Now, you might consider it rather crass of Casey to be talking about money at a time like this. But we were being intentional about our plans for the future and wanted to do it biblically. God said in Habakkuk 2:2 to write the vision down and make it plain so others could follow it. Well, we had a vision for our life that included a business, and we wanted the Lord to bless it. That's why we were tithing. You see, the first 10 percent of what you make, the Lord says it's His and not to steal from Him. That's described in the book of Malachi, also in the Old Testament. In His Word, the Lord promises that if we obey Him in this, He will bless us beyond measure. I tell you, there's a lot of good stuff in the first part of the Bible.

As a project for a business class, we had to write a marketing plan. So we wrote our vision down, and we both got an A. That it was a joint project was not a problem as the professor allowed that option, and in fact encouraged it as a real-world exercise since most businesses have marketing teams.

Our plan included a joint savings account in which we each deposited whatever we could after our tithes and bills were paid. Because we were honoring the Lord with our "first fruits," as He calls the tithe in the Bible, He blessed the remaining 90 percent of our incomes. It was incredible how much more that 90 percent could accomplish by obeying the Lord. God actually invites us to challenge Him on this promise. Read it for yourself in Malachi, chapter three. He says that He'll pour us out such a big blessing we can barely receive it all. It works! We had over $3,000 saved up in less than three months. But that's not all, wait till I tell you about Dad.

Chapter 17

The Gospel of John 1:1,3,10,12,14 (KJV)

"In the beginning was the Word, and the Word was with God, and the Word was God. All things were made by Him; and without Him was not anything made that was made. He was in the world, and the world was made by Him, and the world knew Him not. But as many as received Him, to them He gave power to become the sons of God, to them that believe on His name: And the Word was made flesh, and dwelled among us, (and we beheld His glory, the glory as of the only begotten of the Father) full of grace and truth."

RIGHT BEFORE GRADUATION, I GOT MY lowest grade in an easy little class called Multi Cultural Communication. All I needed to complete my degree was two credits. I took this podunkety, no test required, easy peasy course and nearly flunked it.

The very first day, the middle-aged, slightly plump professor, who was neatly dressed in a button-down collar and tie, proclaimed, "I will not tolerate any sexist, homophobic, racist, or religious bigotry in my class! We're all animals out of the same f - - - ing cesspool, right?"

I don't know about the other students, but I was shocked at his f-bomb. I like to sit in the front row, it makes me pay attention. He was standing right in front of me when he expected us all to be so impressed by his foul language and obediently agree about our less than human heritage.

I immediately spoke up, "Nope."

"Nope, what?" he looked perplexed.

"Nope, I'm not an animal. I'm a born again, Bible believing, Holy Ghost filled, Jesus following daughter created in the image of the Living God." As he took a breath and turned as red as my own freckles, I added, "And I'm not afraid of homosexuals, people of varying skin pigment, or believers in other faiths. As a Christian, I'm called to love everybody, including professors with potty mouths."

And that's how Mr. Conway got the nickname "Professor Potty Mouth."

As he crushed the erasable marker in his fist, our teacher leaned over with his hands on my desk and growled, "See me after class."

When the clock registered time to leave, several students lined up to talk to him. I quickly stuffed my notes and textbook in my backpack and stood up. He glared at me. I sat back down.

Finally, the class was empty, and he slowly intoned, as if I were stupid, "I. Will. Not. Tolerate. Religious. Fanatics."

"Okay, good," I responded. "Don't care much for religion, myself. I like the way you explained how we're to be tolerant of different points of view. Glad to know I'm free to think for myself. By the way, the word phobic denotes fear. So no Christian phobia, either, right?"

Believe, me, I worked hard for those two little credits. I turned in all the assignments on time and never missed a class. Mostly a writing and discussion course, I quoted from the Bible and Bible scholars in my essays. I interjected my Christian perspective without being strident during roundtable sharing. This earned me mediocre grades, but I had a blast. Once after class, another student came up to me walking out the building and said that his dad was a pastor and he was thinking of going back to church. Another one, during a small group discussion on abortion and mercy killing, shyly agreed with me about human life being sacred.

The class pet, however, pushed past me as we exited the room another day, and quoted Karl Marx, "Religion is the opium of the people."

His sneer faltered when I responded with, "Funny, Marx's totalitarian religion of Communism didn't seem to make him very happy. He suffered for years from depression and died at 64 of a lung ailment after a life of heavy drinking, partying, and chain smoking. Having tried some of that stuff, I've found that God's love is a better way of coping. You might want to try it. Have a blessed day!"

Dressed in my favorite black and white "Not Today, Satan" T-shirt, I left him stammering as I went on my way, hoping something might penetrate past prejudice and pride.

Now here's the real kicker. I encountered Professor Potty Mouth days after turning in my final paper. Since I was all done, I didn't have to attend the last class, which was for students to make up missed assignments. Anyway, he was crossing campus, and we intersected. I told him I really enjoyed his class. He looked flushed and disheveled. I asked him if he was okay. He said he had a lot of stress. (In class he once referred to his live-in girlfriend as a b....!) So much for sexist language phobia.

Anyway, I offered, "Can I pray for you?"

He gave me a funny look and shrugged, "Sure, why not? What harm can it do?" He didn't wait for me to launch into prayer as I expected but continued on his way. I prayed out loud for him right then and there to know the peace of Lord Jesus. He stopped, looked back, and said, "Yes, I need it." With a dismissing wave he was off. This, after his much earlier pronouncement in class that he was an avowed atheist. I never saw him again. I still pray for him.

The class didn't really affect my grade point average. And who cares? I was graduating. I think that that C stands for courage, and I wear it as a badge of honor. To suffer for Christ is gain.

Now that Casey and I were done with school, it was time to seriously put the rest of God's plan for us together. We got married.

We started a business out of a friend's garage. We got pregnant. Yes, in that order.

Our wedding was simple. We didn't want to spend a lot of money on a one-day event when we had a lifetime to bank for. Mom was cool with it. Dad gave us a choice. Five thousand dollars toward a wedding or a check of the same. We took the money.

Casey's family met me for the first time in Sheila's backyard where the little ceremony and reception were held. His mom lived in South Florida and rarely made the trip up to our part of the state. She lived with Casey's sister, who took care of her and brought her up with a wheelchair. The only thing I could see wrong with her was that she was seriously obese and sad. I guess she missed Casey's dad, who had passed away a few years before. I wish I could've met him.

Casey had taken Marcus down to see his grandmother and aunt whenever he could. Aunt Sissy obviously loved them both and took charge of Marcus at our wedding in his new outfit with a bright blue bow tie that matched his dad's. I really appreciated my future sister-in-law pitching in at this hectic time. Unfortunately for her, Casey's mother seemed disinterested in everything but herself. Even during our vows, administered by Paul, she kept on about her own misery and missed a lot of the sweet moments. Mom thought she was rude. My heart hurt for my husband, who so wanted his mom to have a good time. I remember her saying to me, with a pointing finger, "You'd better be good to my son." She even called his ex-girl-friend a bad name in front of Marcus. It took me a while, but God later helped me understand and forgive my mother-in-law.

Besides having the man of my dreams, the best part of our wedding was my dad. He and June had driven over in a new BMW and stayed at a motel. Dad looked a lot older, but in a nice, distinguished way. June has always been a sweety. You can tell she really loves him. She was polite and respectful to mom. Dad was merely civil, until June poked him and said, "You both can be very proud of Marney, today. She's turned out amazing!"

Mom told me about this later. I was too busy greeting our other guests, friends from church, my lady I take care of and her daughter, and Casey's co-workers. Sheila's mom and dad were there too. And guess who else? Remember Sheila's brother, John? Yes, he'd come back home from New Mexico with his tail between his legs, kinda like me. He was trying to get back in college and started attending our church. At first, I felt pretty embarrassed at seeing him, remembering what a mess I was back then. But he didn't bring it up, thank the Lord.

As wedding planner, Sheila had enlisted her family and our church friends in doing a lot of the work for our big day. They rented folding chairs and tables, decorated with real flowers, and made the food, which was wonderful. The cake was homemade, in the shape of a car. Sheila thought of everything.

We wrote our own vows. They followed the outline Paul gave in Ephesians about husbands loving their wives like Christ loved the Church, giving himself for her. And for my part, it was to respect my husband as I obey God. No one had to tell me to love Casey with my whole soul. What I learned to remember as the years rolled on was to defer to him whenever we disagreed. I'd just let it go, offer him up to the Lord if I thought he was wrong and say, "Okay, God, he's your kid. You deal with him." We avoided a lot of fights that way. And as Casey learned how much I respected him by not nagging at him, he loved me more and more. The more he loved me, the more I respected him. We had a beautiful marriage, full of grace.

After a long handshake at the end of the reception, Dad handed Casey a large envelope. A couple days before, Casey and I had presented our business plan to him. In the envelope was the business plan with his comments and suggestions written on it. Plus, a check. Suddenly, we knew that we'd be moving our business out of that garage and into a real shop much sooner than we'd figured. I guess Dad liked the plan a lot. The check was for a lot. This was in addition to the $5,000, too.

When it came time to say goodbye to Dad and June, Casey shook his hand again and asked if he could call him in the future for more advice. That done, we all hugged and kissed, and they drove off. Casey and I took Marcus to Orlando for his first Disney foray.

Having a five-year-old on your honeymoon can be a lot of fun. We'd tire him out so that he'd go to bed early and then, well, then we'd be alone in our two-bedroom suite. Oh, my! Being with Casey was a whole new experience fashioned by the freedom of real marital love. Discovering each other after having waited heightened our joy as we relished the luxury of our God-bonded life together.

Chapter 18

Ephesians 2:8, 9 (NIV)

"For it is by grace you have been saved, through faith—and this is not from yourselves, it is the gift of God—not by works, so that no one can boast."

AS I PREPARED TO HAVE A BABY AFTER quickly becoming pregnant following our honeymoon, Casey built a business of doing high-end automotive restorations. Nicknamed "Bondoman" for his gift of applying body putty to make seamless repairs to car panels, my husband hired two young guys from church and Gary, an older, very experienced body man to help with the tear down, part replacement, and myriad other jobs of sanding, cleaning, and generally preparing the cake for the icing. (Read: paint spraying.)

The spraying he left to Gary, who was also a talented air brush artist. Casey was himself still learning the fine art of dancing around a car with a pneumatic spray gun without getting tangled in the air hose or causing drips, fisheyes, or any other blemishes with costly, cantankerous automotive paint.

Word got around, and soon we had a lineup of jobs from rich, retired car lovers. Casey worked like a maniac. I did the books, billing and ordering, kept our garage liability insurance up to date, and answered the phone. The shop was always presentable. Tools got cleaned and neatly put up for the next job. The floor in the brightly lit paint booth was kept free of dust and debris. Casey took pride in showing new customers the workspaces and ongoing projects. His reputation grew, which proved to be a challenge.

At only 26 years old, my ambitious man faced off with his biggest enemy: pride. I wasn't much help in this regard, as I was extremely proud of him. I'd brag about how amazing he was and how well the business was going. Casey would warn me, saying, "Cut it out, Marney. You're going to get me in trouble." But, come on, he enjoyed the praise.

Sure enough, six months after our baby's arrival, trouble came. Our beautiful girl, named Cecilia after Casey's sister (nicknamed Sissy), got a serious lung infection that required her to be hospitalized with IV antibiotics. I panicked. I did not want my baby on mega doses of drugs. I also didn't want her to be sick. During this time, Casey's mother had a heart attack and was in the hospital with dire predictions of her survival. This tore my husband up. He sped up and down the freeway from one hospital to another. Because of his absence, although brief, our business suffered. One of the apprentices we employed neglected to properly dispose of some used automotive fluids right as the EPA inspector came around. This resulted in a big fine and would never have happened if Casey had been present. He blamed himself for this.

One late night, hours after he'd driven nearly 400 grueling miles from South Florida where his mom hovered in and out of consciousness, we just held each other in bed. Our pretty world seemed to be crashing down around us. We were overwhelmed, looking at all the problems. Casey had driven straight to Cecilia's hospital room where Mom and I'd been keeping vigil for days. We left Mom there and dragged ourselves home at her insistence.

We had a house mortgage to pay, hospital bills loomed, along with a backlog of jobs. It was all I could do to keep my OCD husband from spending the night working his tail off at the garage without any sleep. Around 3:00 a.m., I woke to hear him praying. I slid off the bed and knelt beside his bent form. I wanted to rail against the attack on my family. With his deep voice softly entreating, Casey asked God to forgive him for his pride. He did not blame God. He repented. He asked the Lord to cleanse him of leaning upon his own human strength instead of on Jesus's loving provision.

This is what he said: "Father God, I thank you for correcting me. I receive your tender mercy with gratitude on behalf of my family. Lord, my reputation, my righteousness is filthy rags. If I don't live this life to give You glory, to show others Your powerful sufficiency, then I've wasted it. I'm releasing it all to You, dear God. I believe You and trust You because You're good and all powerful. You love us. So, in the name of Your son, Jesus Christ, I proclaim victory as a testimony to Your great love for us, Your little children. Bless You, wonderful Savior. Bless Your Holy Name. I give You praise and honor and glory. Show Yourself mighty, Lord. In the authority You gave us in Jesus's name, I call our baby girl completely healed and my mom in Your divine care. Amen."

I caught on and prayed in the same vein, instead of whining and begging like I felt, but giving honor to God in our trial. Peace flowed into our hearts. Casey remained on his knees long after I went back to bed. Before dawn, he finally eased under the covers and drifted away as we clung to each other.

My cell went off around eight next morning. I quickly shut it off not wanting it to wake Casey. I called Sheila back from the kitchen. "Marney!" she blurted. "Cecilia's going to be all right. Last night, Paul and I prayed and prayed, and we got such a peace about her. Everything's going to be all right!"

Turns out, they woke about the same time we did to pray. Our friends interceding for us panned out. I called Mom, who had remained in our daughter's hospital room all that night. She said that Cecilia's fever broke around three after a major crisis. The duty nurse and Mom held hands and prayed. She said right after that our little darling woke up, coughed, and took a clear breath, her blue eyes fixed on the ceiling. You may say it was the medicine. I know it was God.

All that next day, Casey and I were inseparable. We held Cecilia and rejoiced at the prognosis of a complete recovery and prediction she'd be home soon. We went by the shop. Worship music was playing, and Gary had not only our two apprentices on the job, but there were two more kids there. Cody, the one who messed up, had his girlfriend tidying up. Another friend of his was there, too, detailing a finished 1950 Chevy pickup.

Cody explained, "I'm so sorry about the fine, Casey. You don't have to pay me this week or my friends. You're an awesome boss. We all just wanted to help you get caught up."

Later that day, the Chevy owner came by to get his truck and was so happy with the restoration, he tipped us an extra $300. This after Casey told him about how good the Lord was for healing our daughter. Not only was the brightly flamed orange truck beautiful, but it got done a day ahead of schedule, thanks to our amazing crew.

Two Sundays later, we were able to bring Cecilia to church. It was a happy, sad day. Sissy had called the night before. Casey's mom had passed away. By God's grace, earlier that week, when Casey drove down to see her, he led their mother into the Kingdom by praying with her when she was lucid. Knowing that this self-centered, defeated woman accepted the Lord's salvation almost at the last minute gave Casey great relief and joy. Sissy said she drifted off with a sweet smile. So after church, we left Cecilia with Mom and drove down for the funeral.

I learned my lesson. You don't play around with God. Never take His blessings for granted. He wants us to give Him the credit for everything good in our lives. When we claim our success is due to our own efforts, we forget that He's the one Who makes all things possible. Sure, we apply ourselves when opportunities come. But it's God and only God Who supplies us with our talents, our abilities, and the people in our lives who assist us. As the Apostle Paul says in the fourth chapter of Philippians, "My God will supply all your needs according to His riches in glory by Christ Jesus." Another good thing to remember is found in Proverbs 15:33. "Humility comes before honor."

To be perfectly honest, I'm still really proud of my husband. Or maybe it's better said that I appreciate him even more after the way his faith grew during this ordeal. But later on, I would learn that I can't lean on someone else's faith. I have to work my own. You'll see.

Chapter 19

John 10:27–30 (NIV)

"My sheep listen to My voice; I know them, and
they follow Me. I give them eternal life, and they
shall never perish; no one will snatch them out of
My hand. My Father, who has given them to me, is
greater than all; no one can snatch them out of My
Father's hand. I and the Father are one."

SHEILA'S LITTLE BOY, DAVID, AND OUR
little girl grew up together as close as cousins. We eventually bought
a bigger home near Sheila and Paul, who had the foresight to get
a three-bedroom house to begin with. After David, Sheila gave
birth to a little girl they aptly named Serenity. Cecelia and Serenity
became best friends. We were godparents to one another's children,
with Marcus as the eldest. Casey made an irresistible offer to Sue,
his ex. Without having to go to court, they agreed that Casey would
continue sending her funds equivalent to the child support she'd
been getting until Marcus turned 18. In exchange, Casey and I got
full custody, and Sue got him on the occasional weekend and holiday. Although, in her way, she certainly loved her son, that suited
her freewheeling lifestyle just fine.

We later learned that Sue had an abortion when Marcus was
little. This came to light when our son started dating in high school.
He and three other kids were in a car wreck coming back from a

movie late one night. Marcus's date was injured with a fractured leg. Marcus, the driver, and his girlfriend were bruised and scared. The police report came back finding the driver just barely below the alcohol limit, so he didn't go to jail, but he did get in major trouble. Anyway, when Sue found out about it, she exploded. This pillar of moral prudence railed against our son about having sex and getting a girl pregnant and needing to get an abortion. Somehow, during her tirade, no doubt intended as a wise warning, Sue blurted out that she'd had to do that, herself.

Understand, please, that we'd taught our kids to be followers of biblical truth and trusted Marcus to have a strong foundation for self-control. He'd shown us no reason to doubt him until this accident. Casey and I were dismayed that he was in a car with a kid who'd been drinking. It turned out that Marcus didn't know about the bottle in the front seat. Right before the start of his senior year, finding out that his sibling had been "terminated" threw him into a tailspin, not to mention the horror of seeing his girlfriend taken away in an ambulance.

It was a major wake up for us all. Casey called a halt to life as we routinely knew it. He arranged for the shop, now at a larger location and expanded to include 16 employees, collision, upholstery, and custom recreational vehicles, to run without us for two weeks. Since it was summer, we loaded all the kids into a motor home and headed up to North Carolina for a mountain retreat. Sheila, Paul, and Mom joined us a few days later.

Sitting out on the rental cabin deck overlooking a verdant mountain forest around sunset, Marcus opened up. I'd just brought out some snacks to join my husband and our son, both reclining in Adirondack chairs with matching long legs stretched out before them. They looked so much alike, especially since Casey had lost the beard some years ago. Even their speech inflexions mirrored their thoughtfully laid-back body language.

I set the food down on a plastic table. The girls and David were on the deck below playing ping pong. Sheila, Paul, and Mom were arriving the next day, so I had meals on my mind. But digesting

Marcus's realizations shifted my brain off groceries and onto God's sovereign grace.

"I knew it was going to happen," Marcus said, referring to the accident. "Right before we got in the car as we left the theater, I heard a voice telling me to call you, Dad, and have you pick Marcie and me up."

Giving his son a chance to continue, Casey propped his feet up on the deck rail and crossed his ankles. Marcus mimicked the action, without even thinking, I'm sure. I wanted to blurt out, "You did? Really!" but I held my breath and my tongue.

"It's all my fault Marcie got hurt" Marcus reflected. "I should've listened. I know it was God, or an angel, or something trying to warn me. But I didn't want to look stupid in front of my friends, so I brushed it off." He slapped his forehead. "I'm so sorry, Dad."

"Well now, let's consider this a moment, Son," Casey answered. "Hearing from God or an angel or something is a pretty big deal. This ever happen to you before?"

Marcus furrowed heavy black brows and just said, "Nope."

Casey voiced a low hum, almost a growl, his thinking sound.

"I guess I'm going to obey that voice if I ever hear it again," Marcus offered.

"It's a matter of trust, isn't it?" Casey returned. "The Lord loves you, and He's completely capable of communicating with us. The trick is to know if it's His voice and not some other."

Boy, oh boy, am I ever a witness to that, I thought but held my peace.

"Since the warning proved to be accurate," Casey continued, "I'd say you heard from almighty God, all right."

"Yes, sir, I do believe I did," Marcus took a deep breath of relief.

"Okay, so here's the deal, Son. You know it's from God if it agrees with His Word, the Bible, if it's comforting, truthful, and builds you up in some pure way." Casey switched his crossed ankles and reached for corn chips. "If those criteria are met, then we'd best obey that voice."

Marcus hum-growled, put his feet on the deck, leaned over to the table to grab a cookie, and resumed his foot perched position, swapping ankles.

I finally entered the conversation while they chewed. "Have you heard from Marcie today?"

"Yeah," Marcus muttered as he munched. "She's home and doing a lot better. But she's grounded."

Marcie's parents, also friends of ours at church, had seemed happy that she was dating our son, who was on the youth worship team. Evidently, they'd decided to rein in their daughter, and I couldn't blame them. I resolved to call them in the morning.

"But, come on, I mean, how could Mom (referring to Sue, of course) think I'd be getting Marcie pregnant?" Marcus stood up and walked over to the other end of the deck. He flapped his arms, turned around, and plunked back down on the chair before snagging another cookie. "And how could she? I mean, she just threw that out about the abortion like it was . . . I don't know. Like it was the thing to do when you don't want to have a baby!"

That brought me back, I can tell you. The abortion issue. Pure selfishness, I thought. What was nine months of sacrifice when another person's entire existence hung in the balance? Especially with so many people waiting to adopt. But after thinking this, I felt convicted. I was judging Sue. Abortion, I knew, was no good answer to an unplanned pregnancy. But hating someone for it was just as bad. Jesus even said that being angry with someone is like murdering them in your heart.

"You need to pray for God to help you forgive her," I offered, prompted by Holy Spirit.

That brought both their heads up. Casey nodded and said, "She's right, Marcus. If you don't forgive your mother, it'll just cause a root of bitterness to grow in you. What's done is done. She may have sinned. But don't let the devil lead you into the sin of unforgiveness as a reaction to her tragic decision."

It was dark, and the night crickets were chirping. A bird called. The crickets hushed. Even the leaves stilled. Marcus extended his hands to each of us. We prayed. He cried. We hugged him. The crickets started back up, a fresh breeze rustled through the trees, and an owl hooted. Then the other kids came out onto our deck, claiming they were starving to death. I went in to fix sandwiches and thanked the dear Lord for our precious children, truly a blessing from God.

Chapter 20

Job 12:7–10 (NIV)

"But ask the animals, and they will teach you, or the birds in the sky, and they will tell you; or speak to the earth, and it will teach you, or let the fish in the sea inform you. Which of all these does not know that the hand of the Lord has done this? In His hand is the life of every creature and the breath of all mankind."

WITH SHEILA, PAUL, AND MOM FINALLY there, we managed a special outing almost every day. We went rafting on the Tennessee River, took our mirth-filled motor home to Table Rock where we perched near the precipice for pictures, and camped one night. It took two whole days to do Dolly Wood. Everyone loved the horseback ride through the foothills of the Smokies near Cherokee. Now in her early 50s, Mom was still game for just about anything. I think my favorite thing was the river. I love nature, as you know. Following the bends brought surprises with each graceful turn of the mighty dark blue water. Our guide kept us safe so we could really enjoy the scenery, which culminated by the Fontana Dam. This afforded a valuable history lesson for the kids, who learned about the Great Depression, the Civilian Corps of Engineers, and the formation of much of the infrastructure of our nation during a troubled time.

Casey's favorite thing was the steam engine train ride. The man loves motors, and this one was big, noisy, stinky, and really cool. It included lunch in an eighteenth-century dining car, a scary, dark length of tunnel, and amazing mountain vantage points. We learned about Civil War history as the area was replete with battle lore. It was an exciting, sobering, and unforgettable foray for all of us, especially the boys (grown and small).

We were sad to see Sheila and Paul go. They took their kids and Mom with them, leaving just the four of us for the remaining three days. The big cabin perched above a deep gulch seemed like home by then. We were content to just hang out, take little walks, and be with one another. It was an important healing time for Marcus, who needed to be with his family. Even though on the cusp of full-blown adulthood, our teenager needed to cleave closer to us. Before long, he'd be gone, out on his own with the solid foundation of family and faith. Each evening, we had a little Bible reading and devotion. Marcus and Cecilia enjoyed this as much as we did, especially since Marcus had brought his guitar. We all loved singing the praise and worship songs from church.

That last Sunday, we had our own little early service before hitting the road for home. Evidently, our neighbors enjoyed it too. A brown mama bear and her two cubs lingered on the forest floor not far from the cabin. As we sang and prayed, they watched from below the bottom deck, sitting on their haunches and sniffing the praise filled air. I've got pictures to prove it! The Bible speaks about even the trees clapping their hands at the praise of the Lord. I believe it.

We all hit the floor running back in Florida but with renewed and rested souls. The kids went back to school. Casey and I were hard at work. After speaking with Marcie's parents about the car accident and the dating situation, things settled down there, as well. We all agreed that from now on, Marcus would do the driving on double dates. They affirmed their trust in him, since Marcie's story jived with Marcus's about not drinking that night. We watched their blossoming romance with reserved hope.

As Mom put it, "Why, they're adorable together. Quit worrying you two, and let the kids find their way. Marcus knows he can come to you to discuss anything. You can trust that boy because you raised him right!"

The following winter, I was generating invoices, getting ready for tax time, and composing a budget when my pen rolled under the desk. Even though we clean the shop before closing each night, you just can't get rid of all the dust in a body shop. Regularly changing air conditioning filters and blowing out commercial ventilation systems is a must. Still, I was surprised at what I found on the floor down there. Dust, dust bunnies, a (thankfully) dead palmetto bug (for you Northerners, it is a *gigantic* cockroach), and something else.

After I shook the dirt off the crumpled piece of paper and swept up with the rest, I smoothed it out to read: "In this world you will have trouble. But take heart! I have overcome the world."

Recognizing this verse from the Gospel of John, I wondered how the note got there. It's not my habit to throw God's Word on the floor. I showed it to Casey as we ate lunch with some of the crew at our favorite barbeque place.

"Oh, yeah, I guess it fell out of my notebook when you were in Texas," he said.

I'd taken Cecilia with me to Austin to be with Dad and June while my stepmom was in the hospital. A mammogram resulted in early detection of breast cancer, and so she had to have a lumpectomy. I was happy to go when Dad called. I found out that June had requested me to be there for his sake. Seeing my father weakened by worry over his wife made me realize that he needed support, too. June is a wise, unselfish woman. But it was Cecilia who really brought up Dad's spirits.

She snuggled her eleven-year-old self up to Grandpa on a couch in the hospital waiting room, took his hand, and asked if he'd pray with her. Big blue eyes entreated him with love and trust. Not much of a believer, he patted her hand and said, "Sure, Baby. I'll listen to you."

Simple prayers are often the best. What matters is the sincerity. God doesn't care about fancy oration. He responds to our hearts. Cecilia tightly closed her eyes and said, "Thank you, Jesus, for helping Grandma and Grandpa know you love them and everything's gonna be okay. Amen."

Daddy was about to let her hand go after responding with a tentative amen, when Cecilia held on tighter and continued, "And show everyone else in this room that you love them, too."

The elderly couple sitting on the other side said, "Amen." Suddenly, we all looked around the room acknowledging one another. There were about eight people there. Each had a story and a need. God knew about us all and cared deeply. A peace curtained the waiting room, covering anxiety and uncertainty. I took a breath and silently thanked the Lord as my father covered Cecilia's hand with his other hand and then looked to me.

"She's something else," was all he said. It was enough for now.

During the week of our stay with Dad and June, Cecilia kept up with her schoolwork, due to the kind provision of her teacher. It was during an evening of relaxing in their family room shortly after June was discharged with an encouraging prognosis, that a disturbing item about my child's education came to light.

Dad had asked her what her favorite class was. She answered English because she liked reading stories. Then he asked what her least favorite class was. The answer shocked us.

Eyes downcast, in a whisper, she said, "Sex education class."

Sex education for my child just starting middle school? And I wasn't consulted about it?

Dad was flabbergasted. June looked up from her knitting, concerned. While I tried to rein in my fears, she softly inquired, "And what are they teaching you in sex education class, dear?"

Over the next ten minutes, without unduly embarrassing my child, June gently extracted the following information. In a coeducational setting, advertised to us parents as "health education," kids were being taught that sexuality was meant to be enjoyed and that the potentially hazardous result of it, pregnancy, can easily be prevented with birth control pills. I cringed at the thought of messing with developing endocrine systems of little girls. But it got worse.

The children were handed questionnaires about their sexuality and whether or not they actually thought they were the gender assigned to them at birth! I asked what happened to those questionnaires.

"Oh, teacher collected them," she said.

Right then I was ready to dial the school and demand to see my child's questionnaire. Again, June intervened by asking, "And did teacher explain what happens when a student decides they are in the wrong sex?"

Cecilia's answer was so low, I had to lean in to hear her. "I don't know. I guess that's when they see the nurse. And teacher talked about bathrooms." She looked up and favored me with a shadow of a grin, "I don't want to be a boy. I'm glad I'm a girl. I won't have to go to the nurse."

My head exploded. Dad shook his in disbelief and said, "My God, what is the world coming to?"

June just said, "We're glad you're a girl, too, sweetie. You're our precious little princess, and someday you'll meet your Prince Charming. And after you two get married, then you can love each other, and God will bless you with your own wonderful family."

"Oh, good," Cecilia answered. "I don't like pills, and I don't like the kids who're always taking them. They act weird. Mommy, can I go to my room and do my homework now?"

She bounced out of the room, glad to have this uncomfortable disclosure done.

What did that mean, other kids always taking pills? Were there drug addicts in the sixth grade? My mind was reeling. I had to go for a walk to clear it. I started along the perimeter of the fancy gated community around sunset. It was full dark when I returned. I had prayed, rehearsed my speeches with the school board and Casey. And, of course, I called Sheila.

"That's why we decided to homeschool our kids," Sheila said. "Remember, I told you about some of the sketchy things being taught in public school? There's the obvious problem of Darwinism. Ridiculous! Since when has anyone ever seen one species come out of another one. And then there's the problem with the way they're teaching American history. Total denial of the Christian roots of our founders. I could go on and on."

I knew she was right. But how could I homeschool when I was so busy with work?

Sheila, naturally, had the answer for that, too. "You can do what we do. We network with other homeschoolers. We share classroom time, resources, outings, all kinds of things. David and Serenity love it. The other thing you could consider is private Christian school. We may go that way soon, ourselves. You've heard about Family Faith Fellowship starting one up in January. Why not enroll Cecilia there?"

We talked about the pros and cons of educational options and concluded that it was a matter for earnestly seeking the Lord. After praying with Sheila, I called Casey. He had just picked Marcus up from basketball practice. As they ate pizza and with Casey's phone on speaker, the three of us reviewed the realities of public school. Marcus insisted that he wanted to stay the course and finish where he was. However, he agreed that it might be better for his little sister to be where she'd be more protected.

I sat down on the guest bed next to Cecilia where she was sprawled out, answering questions in a math workbook. As soon as I asked her about the possibility of enrolling in a different kind of school, she sat up and hugged me.

"Yes, Mommie, pleeeze! I don't want to be where kids don't even know if they're supposed to be boys or girls. It's so creepy!"

That settled it. Almost.

Chapter 21

Daniel 6:19-20 (NIV)

"At the first light of dawn, the king got up and hurried to the lions' den. When he came near the den, he called to Daniel in an anguished voice, 'Daniel, servant of the living God, has your God, whom you serve continually, been able to rescue you from the lions?'"

MY TIME IN TEXAS WAS PRODUCTIVE ON several counts. I grew closer to Dad, who seemed more inclined to trust Jesus, thanks to his granddaughter. June taught me patience by the gentle way she got Cecilia to open up. Casey and I agreed that we'd transfer Cecilia to a Christian school. She came home to Florida happier, knowing she was going to be in classes with her church friends starting next semester. Marcus got to be in on an adult discussion in which he was able to voice his preferences about his schooling. The way in which he addressed our concerns demonstrated his maturity and increased our trust. Marcus also revealed adult understanding when he weighed in on the decision about Cecilia's education.

Finally, I drafted a stinging letter to the school board, which led me on a course I could not have imagined. Politics. Hoo boy!

You may be wondering why I'd do such a foolish thing. But I felt urged by Holy Spirit. If Christians don't get into public discussion and policy making, then it falls to people who don't hold the morals and principles taught in God's Word. And how's that working, folks? Think about it.

I ran for school board in the next election on a platform of Christian values, including teaching good old-fashioned abstinence, instead of birth control for youngsters, and biology that included human development from conception. Plus, I advocated religious freedom for the campuses. At this time, Bible study had been banned at several schools.

I lost. But my God-inspired candidacy sparked a conversation, among other things. Casey's business got spray-painted "religious bigot." I received hate mail. The following election, an energetic young minister who caught the vision succeeded in getting elected to the school board. Also, two Christian county commissioners won seats, one of them a popular local plumber. Yup, Paul caught the fever and ran on a platform promoting biblical principles. Some folks cultivate the ground, some plant, and others harvest. But the ground all belongs to God, you know? I guess I whacked out a few weeds, clearing the way a bit.

I can't say at this point that these advances for the cause of sanity totally changed the tide. But at least it kept the dam holding back pigsty culture from busting loose and overrunning our community completely. Eventually, after-hours Bible studies were allowed in the schools and abstinence was included, along with birth control, in the sex ed class. A terrible proposed county ordinance outlawing Christian counseling for people struggling with same sex attraction got narrowly defeated by the county commission, thanks in large part to Paul. He argued, why limit the options for people who don't want to be confused about their sexuality? "If folks want Bible-based counseling, let 'em have it, for Pete's sake!" A big advocate of personal freedom, Paul's winning slogan became "Let 'em have it!"

I believe that painting over a bit of graffiti and sweetly responding "Jesus bless you" to hate mail was a small price to pay and well worth it. Hello, America.

Throughout it all, God was faithful. Seeing this, our faith grew stronger as we each reached toward whatever God had next and persevered past the enemy's obstacles along the way. I became involved as a volunteer in the administration of Christian Academy, our school at Family Faith Fellowship, which Sheila and Paul's kids also attended. Marcus graduated high school and went on to college where he continued Jesus culture outreach through his Christian fraternity. Paul sold his business and went into full-time ministry with Sheila by his side, as well as serving four terms on the county commission. Casey's business continued to prosper because he made a point to glorify God by supporting Christian causes, hiring and training at-risk youth, and practicing sound ethics professionally. We weren't always successful, but we kept the faith, encouraging one another that God's righteous promises would see us through.

Everyone knows that Florida is a great place to live. Low taxes, sunny climate, and beautiful beaches makes it so desirable that thousands move into the state each month. There is diversity of culture in many parts. Our area in the middle of the top still displays Southern culture. By that, I mean people are friendly, hospitable, and largely Christian. There are churches everywhere. Not all of them teach the full gospel of Jesus Christ. Some have given place to popular culture, accepting same-sex marriage and other practices that contradict the Bible. But still, you'll find that believers of these many stripes generally care about people, our community, and the world at large.

This became evident the September that followed our twentieth wedding anniversary. Hurricane Harry hit.

The weather map looked ominous. This deadly cat-five storm was headed right for us from the Gulf of Mexico. Just brushing by, it had already torn at the fringes of Texas and Louisiana. Marcus, now 25, engaged to Marcie and starting out in his chosen profession, dentistry, showed up the week before. Together, he, Casey, Paul, and David busied themselves hammering plywood over neighborhood windows and trimming tree branches away from roofs. Mom, who came to live with us when Marcus moved out, Cecilia, Sheila, Serenity, and I filled containers of water, stood in line for gasoline, and packed emergency kits. The day before Hurricane Harry was sure to hit our coast, we were still undecided about evacuating or riding it out. One thing for sure, we were in it together.

It was Serenity who captured the spirit of the moment best as we congregated in Sheila's family room. "I have a weird peace about this whole thing," she began. "At first, I was scared, looking at the storm path predictions. But then I remembered how Jesus rebuked the storm. He said we could do whatever He did if we did it in His name. I want us to rebuke this storm, not to make ourselves great, but to show that Jesus is."

This excited me. I remembered back when Casey and I were first dating and meeting at Sheila and Paul's. Remember the lesson about eagles? They fly *toward* the storm to soar above it. Isn't that what intercessory prayer is? I wanted to shout! "Yes, let's take a stand and show the way God lifts us above the storm!"

Paul, now sporting a salt-and-pepper goatee, stroked his mustache and frowned thoughtfully at his daughter. Casey did his bass hum-growl thing, followed by Marcus's perfectly matched rumble. I wanted to sing out in soprano, "Let's pray, ya'll!"

Sheila just clasped her hand in her daughter's and said, "Serenity, do what the Lord calls you to."

This cute and normally shy high school senior began her prayer quietly thanking Father God for the power of the Holy Ghost in Jesus's name. Immediately, the triune God of Heaven filled the room. We all prayed in turn, even Cecilia and Mom. As the prayers circled around and around the room, we got excited. Pretty soon we were shouting past the ceiling and waving our arms, calling the storm out, and telling it to skedaddle!

True to my radical nature, I grabbed Sheila's hand and tugged her to the door. A moment later, we were all out on the front yard yelling at the sky and telling Satan where he could put it, right back out in the gulf and away from Florida.

Now, you're probably thinking. Hoo boy! You people are crazy!

Yes, I'm crazy by worldly standards. I'm crazy enough to stand in the rain and speak to a storm but not on my own. I stand upon the rock of Jesus Christ, and I believe in His saving power. He's a miracle worker. He said in James chapter four, "You have not because you ask not." Jesus told His disciple to ask in order to receive. The trick is to do it in faith, to expect it even when you don't see it.

The wind picked up as we poured out our hearts. It howled back at us, a snarling warning of what was to come. But we persisted. We kept it up until neighbors noticed. The elderly couple next door, who had decided to wait the story out, joined in. Then the folks across the street, nice quiet Baptists, grinning sheepishly came over, too. But the funniest thing of all was when our politically correct atheist gay professor couple came out with pots and metal spoons and started banging!

As the cacophony increased, Paul began singing "Praise God from Whom All Blessings Flow." (My resurrection, born again song, remember?) The rest of us church folk added harmony and, with hands raised and rain coming in sideways, we worshipped and rejoiced. Yup, even the amused skeptics doing percussion sang along. Amazing.

We kept it up until sunset. Soaked and exhilarated, we toweled off and ate tuna fish sandwiches. During the night, the gay guys next door drove off for safety. When we woke up in the morning, it was oddly quiet. Casey turned on the TV. Looking beleaguered and crumpled, the weatherman tried to explain the latest satellite images. I don't understand much about high-pressure and low-pressure systems, myself. But I do know that God worked an undeniable miracle. Harry hiked back out to sea and fizzled after another three days.

Soon afterward, I got this picture in my head, which I believe was a download from God. It was of an angel, standing over Florida leaning forward with his arms on his hips and blowing. The sun, brightly cresting behind him, illuminated angry, retreating clouds skewered with lightning. I painted it. It now hangs in the cafeteria of Christian Academy with a sign that says, "Call upon the Lord and expect a miracle!"

Chapter 22

Ephesians 2:10 (NIV)

"For we are God's handiwork, created in Christ Jesus to do good works, which God prepared in advance for us to do."

CASEY ENJOYED HIS WORK SO MUCH, that even after closing time he had a hankering to get creative with some of the junk that tends to pile up around the back of a body shop. One night I watched as he wheeled the frame of a 1200 Goldwing into the welding room. Next, he pushed a Saturn Ion behind it that had been rear-ended and totaled. Observing another person thinking is pretty entertaining. He stood staring at the two objects, walked around them a few times, pursed his lips, grunted, and called it a day.

At this point, both our kids were on their own. I'd just turned 50. Empty nesting isn't so bad when you have someone to do stuff with. However, at this point, besides work, church, and daily life, Casey and I really didn't have a unique activity we shared. Mom was nearing the bend to 70 and still living with us, but increasingly content to just hang out at home, read, and go with friends to lunch or shopping.

My husband and I were lying face up, side by side in bed this night when I asked Casey what he was going to do with the motorcycle frame and car. He took a deep breath, turned to look at me lovingly, and said, "I'm making something fun for us to do together, Red."

I loved it when he called me Red. No one else ever did, especially not at this stage when my bright hair had toned down a few shades with gray. I rolled over to face him, put my hand on his chest and cuddled as he swept me in closer with his strong arm. Before I could think of another question, he was gone, softly snoring away. I left us in that position until my shoulder ached and so turned over, my back along his side. What was his idea of fun? For that matter, what was mine? Pretty soon, I'd drifted off, too. The answer came in the morning.

I woke up to the smell of fresh brewed coffee and my side of the bed dipping under Casey's weight. He handed me a mug after I sat up, grinned, and announced, "I know what to do. It came to me in my sleep. I just couldn't figure it out yesterday, but God showed me."

"Showed you what?" I asked between sips.

"I have to weld the motorcycle frame to the front of the car before I cut it!" he exclaimed, getting animated and almost spilling my coffee. "If I don't, the car'll just do this." He violently gestured downward with his hand and shouted, "*Bam!*"

Before I could figure out what bam meant (would it explode?), he launched off the bed, grabbed his jeans, and shot out the door. I scrambled to catch up, sloshing coffee on my nighty.

By the time I got the office up and running, I was the last one of our crew to reach the welding room in time to see the car with its front bumper stripped, hood discarded, and about to receive another of many welds attaching it to the end of the touring bike frame. A car-motorcycle, otherwise known as our crazy custom trike, was being born.

The first test run was a spectacular success. Casey drove this mangled mess (with some of the wires still sticking out) around the shop.

He'd chopped the car approximately at the steering wheel, completely discarding the passenger compartment and the rest of the vehicle. He locked the rack and pinion steering system so that the front wheels of the front-wheel-drive car became the trike's back wheels to keep them straight. Cables for the car's operating system extended through the new steel reinforced motorcycle frame to reconnect with the Saturn's relocated dash, now installed in the fairing at the front of the bike. The acceleration cable and brake cables connected to the handlebars. The automatic gear shift, relocated from the car, now rested right in front of the temporary motorcycle seat and above the empty space where a bike's gas tank would normally be. The car's gas tank jutted out the back end like a bare butt. It was rough but functional. He even grinned and goosed it on the third drive through the parking lot and performed a wheely as the crew cheered.

The goofy-looking thing had the computer and suspension of a car with the soft buzzing sound of a GMC 2.2-liter motor but much faster pick up due to the reduced weight of the vehicle. I mean, it could boogie!

Over the next weeks, Casey and the boys mounted the car seats, the driver's on the motorcycle frame up front and the passenger's behind and above it on the newly covered car motor. They capped the rear end to house the gas tank by adding the trunk from a wrecked Nissan Altima and went to work on the body, knitting it all together seamlessly with sheet metal and bondo. Those kids got to help with everything as the trike progressed from a mess to a masterpiece.

Over the years, my husband had acquired spray painting expertise and dressed the body in candy apple red of varying hues so that you couldn't tell the exact color as light traveled across it. He had Joyce, our upholstery queen, cover the seats in waterproof black vinyl. She also covered the steps on either side of the passenger seat as well as the narrow floor in front of it in black carpeting. Because of the passenger seat being so high, sitting on top of the car motor, Casey built a second windshield for it. The finishing touch was the prestigious chrome hood ornament off a Jaguar mounted on the Goldwing's front fender. So he could legitimately claim that the trike, which he nicknamed "Red's Ride," was composed of four different vehicles.

Joyce also carpeted the gas tank, which took up half the space of the trunk, and she created a nice clean area in there to carry a small cooler, suitcase, and helmets. When I first rode on it, I felt vulnerable, like I was going to get thrown out, even though I had a seat belt. So Casey constructed sleek compartments on either side of my chair, boxing me in. That's where we kept our rain gear, sunscreen, and goggles. Would you believe he even thought of custom cup holders?

All finished, there remained one last thing. It had to be registered. So we prepared our paperwork for the "Assembled from Parts" vehicle application, loaded the trike onto a car trailer, and headed off to our appointment with the DMV. And that's where we realized God's purpose of the project.

By now, you may be wondering how the Lord fit into this chapter of my story. You've no doubt noticed that the whole purpose of telling you the bad and good things about my little life is to show you how Jesus is *the* way, truth, and life. But what did my talented husband's creation have to do with Jesus? Well, I'll tell you.

Normally, a DMV inspection of a rebuilt salvage or assembled-from-parts vehicle goes like this: the inspector examines the receipts to make sure you didn't steal anything. Then he or she matches up any VIN numbers to make sure you didn't steal anything, barely even looking at the actual vehicle. Then they hand you some more paperwork so you can go to your local tax collector to purchase a new title and registration, proving you didn't steal anything. All this costs money, and I'm not complaining about that. What struck me as odd the first time we went through this process with a rebuilt wrecked car was the actual inspection of the physical, hopefully mechanically sound vehicle. Or should I say, lack of any such practical examination? Like, does it have tires?

In the application, a builder has to address any major component parts as defined in the application. These include the drive train, motor, and transmission. It does not cover what you would think essential parts to make the vehicle safe and road worthy, as in: do the brakes work? In other words, no test drive. Huh?

This wasn't our first rodeo. Casey had purchased a few new wrecked cars at auction that had been branded as salvage (not road worthy), wonderfully fixed them, and then went through the legal yada yada to get them a new title (branded as rebuilt) so they could be sold street legal. Customers loved them. They were getting a practically new car or truck at a greatly reduced price.

Having gone through this strange process before, we just expected the inspector, a lovely young woman named Jerickia, to just glance at the trike to make sure that, yup, it exists, and hand us the paperwork so we could be on our merry way to get the branded title and tag. (That itty bitty motorcycle license plate would look so cute on the back Nissan bumper.)

She must have been new on the job. Jerickia walked out into the parking lot where the trike sat, gleaming bright red on the trailer behind our F250. She stopped midway, flapped her arms (almost losing the paperwork), and then proceeded to climb up on the trailer and actually inspect Red's Ride.

Her favorite part (not on the short list of major component parts) was the sleek, leaping jaguar on the front fender. She stroked it. Then she exclaimed over the second windshield in front of the passenger seat (windshields and seats, also not major component parts). She climbed up into my seat and asked Casey if he'd take her for a ride. What can a rebuilder do? He had that thing unloaded from the trailer before I would ask our perky inspector, "Is this your lunch break?"

By the time they got back from their little joy ride, I was hot and sticky, sitting out in the sun on the edge of the trailer. Was this even legal? I mean, it didn't have a tag yet! And I was hoping to have enough time to get over to the tax collector's office to get one before sunset.

When they returned a few minutes later, Jerickia's black Bantu knots were coming undone and she had an enormous smile on her face. She squealed in delight when Casey cut a wheely as they entered the parking lot. That brought out the other inspector-office-worker-DMV people who all ooed and awed as Casey described the trike's genesis.

A balding guy in a polo shirt asked, "How'd you know where to start?"

"God showed me," Casey replied. Casey went on to explain how he had a dream in which God warned him about not chopping anything until it was securely attached. This led to a discussion of Holy Spirit–inspired dreams and visions. Most of the other people wandered back into the air conditioning, but Jerickia and Baldy stayed. They both had a fascination for God stuff. Before long, Casey invited them out to lunch.

It was over Casey's favorite baby back ribs and sweet tea that we all shared our stories of how the Lord performs in daily life if we just seek Him first. We prayed for Jerickia's grandfather, who was suffering with diabetes. Casey laid hands on Baldy for his ulcers to be healed in Jesus's name. Happy and amazed at the turn this day took, we just barely made it back to our local tax collector before closing. That evening, Casey and I enjoyed our first sunset ride down a country road, relaxed, wind-blown, and street legal.

Chapter 23

Galatians 5:17 (NIV)

"For the flesh desires what is contrary to the Spirit,
and the Spirit what is contrary to the flesh. They
are in conflict with each other, so that you are not
to do whatever you want."

I'M SORRY TO BRING THIS UP, ESPECIALLY
for any young man who happens to read this, but here goes.
Menopause sometimes made me downright ornery. My poor
husband. He didn't quite understand what I was going through.
Normally, I was his happy sidekick, content to do whatever he
wanted. That's because whatever he wanted was creative, fun, and
profitable. Casey just had a solid sense of right to him that made
being around him a joy. Now, that's a gift from God. But me being
bitchy threw him off kilter. He just didn't know how to help me. So
guess what he did?

He called Sheila.

"Well now, Casey," Sheila drawled, "you know Marney's crazy
about you. Problem is, right now she's just, well, crazy."

True to his sex, Casey wanted to simply reach into a tool box,
grab the right solution, and fix me. Done. Back to normal.

But Sheila suggested another tack. "Honey, you keep takin' her
on those motorcycle rides and she'll be just fine. Eventually."

In other words, Sheila was telling him, don't you change just because I had. Stay the course, keep the faith, and press on.

Then Paul got on the phone and reiterated what his wife told my husband. "Yup, she's right, bro. You shoulda seen my sweet darlin' go all cantankerous on me. Ow! Cut it out, Sheila. She just slapped me! But she's back to bein' her dear sweet self again now. Aintcha, baby?"

Casey laughed. They prayed with him to have patience and persevere with the good Lord's help. So that's what he did. We took a lot of sunset rides. This really did help clear my head. I'd just recline a bit in that car seat riding up on top of the softly purring motor like a queen and think about the pretty colored clouds and the moss-draped trees whizzing by. I got a lot of oxygen and reflection on God's goodness.

We'd traverse a familiar circuit that included farm fields, hills, and a gas station/general store where we'd stop for ice cream. It got so that the locals around the station knew us. Sometimes, I'd climb down off my throne and let him take a kid or two for a short spin. They'd buckle up and don one of the helmets, grinning like cute little birds coming out of the egg with a half shell on their heads.

It got to be so that folks thought of Casey as a kind of preacher because he'd always turn the remarks about the awesome contraption into a testimony or story about Jesus. If someone looked anxious or tired or in pain, he'd invariably ask if he could pray for them. A farmer with bad knees actually got healed right on the spot after Casey commanded arthritis to leave in the mighty name of Jesus. The man was still exuberantly squatting and standing by the gas pump as we drove off.

One time we got stopped by the sheriff out in the middle of nowhere.

"You got a registration for this thing?" he demanded gruffly. As I fumbled in my side compartment for it, his partner got out and started circling the bike with her arms crossed. Their dark sunglasses left me clueless and intimidated. I handed him the registration, he hardly even glanced at it, grimaced, and thrust it back at me.

Then Miss Igottabadge perched in front of the trike, pointed at the jaguar, slapped her thigh, and started laughing. *Laughing*! Here I thought we were in for a big ticket for looking weird or speeding or something. Her partner grinned and said, "Man, this thing is so cool! How fast can it go?"

He should've been more considerate of a poor woman suffering from hot flashes.

Anyway, that's how our rides went, Red's Ride was like a calling card, an invitation to a God conversation. The deputies left after Casey and I prayed for them and thanked them for their service. Not their usual traffic stop, right? I can honestly say that not one negative thing came about because of that machine. This includes no actual moving collisions due to other swerving drivers thrusting their phones out their windows videoing us alongside them. That did get scary.

Eventually, my headaches subsided, and I grew more and more attached to these rides. I loved having those broad shoulders out in front of me. I loved the spontaneity of the hundreds of encounters with strangers. I loved Casey's boldness of asking, "Hey, man, can I pray for you?"

We quit working Saturdays and joined a triker club. If they weren't doing an organized ride on weekends, we'd just do our own, go out to breakfast, stop at a park, swim in the springs, and make a day of it. Some of the club members were not Christians, but they just seemed to know that when Casey was around, to mind the swearing. Not that he'd criticize them if they did, but by his conversation, they could tell that he had high standards. The other guys and their partners all liked Casey. They admired his creativity, skill, and unapologetic confidence in Christ. Everyone did.

That brings me to tell you about our neighbors. By this time, we'd sold the big house and moved further out into the country. Mom continued living with us, and we attended the same church, which wasn't too far for her to still meet with friends. But Casey wanted a few acres and a shop at home to play in.

Guess what he bought? Think: field, ditches, dirt driveway, digging up stuff, installing fences, hauling tree limbs, and riding high like a proper yahoo. Yup, Casey went full blown redneck and got himself a shiny new green and yellow John Deere tractor. With implements. Lots of 'em. His hunky JD could put on a bucket, bush hog, cultivator, drag, pallet forks, auger, and potato plow. No, silly, not all at once.

I asked, "You're going to plow potatoes?"

"Never know, Red," he said.

Pretty soon, other folks around us got used to my husband chugging around. First, he offered to mow an elderly couple's field. Before long, he'd helped the guy across the road auger out his post holes (without electrocuting himself when the gate post ran close to the buried electric line), dragged another neighbor's car out of the ditch, and dug a hole for a dead donkey.

Within a few short years of living out there, Casey became the go-to guy for all kinds of things, from banging out little fender dings to welding broken metal lawn furniture to praying for fallen arches.

He also got into fooling around with alternative energy stuff. He built a wood burning furnace that produced a blue flame and wired it to a generator. He messed around with canning jars producing hydrogen. And don't get me started on the magnet motor! I never knew what he'd get into next.

One day, I was just pulling into our driveway with a car full of groceries, when I saw this huge plume of smoke shoot up in front of the shop. I jammed the car in park and ran to find Casey elated, looking up with no eyebrows and his face all black.

"Man! Was that ever cool!" he exulted.

His escapades cemented my belief in guardian angels. I never did understand what my hero was attempting that time. I'm just grateful that no one felt the need to call the sheriff. And whatever might have gone up with the smoke didn't land on anyone's head.

When I attempted to urge Casey to be more cautious, he simply responded by convincing me that I should know how to operate the tractor.

What?

That's right, he told me to climb up there. I did.

By then, I was in my mid 50s and not overly ambitious. But I'm a good sport. I listened as he pointed out the controls, how to raise and lower the bucket and so on, as the diesel motor rumbled so loudly, he had to shout the instructions. The last thing he said before I lurched off was, "Don't grind the gears!"

It was fun. Until I needed to stop. I was heading for a shed and pressed the foot brake. It barely slowed. I was quickly getting closer to disaster when Casey ran after me, flapping his arms and shouting "Clutch! *Clutch*!"

I'm thinking, "Clutch? Why clutch? I don't want to change gears. I want to stop this stupid thing."

The bucket was just about to bash the wall in when an inner voice, one I'd heard years before, you may remember, gently urged, "Just press the clutch down with your left foot."

I did. It stopped immediately.

Seconds later, Casey reached me, sweating and panting. He looked up and grinned. "Put the gear shift in neutral, now. Set the brake and come on down. You did good, Red. Next time, you'll think quicker."

I climbed down, shaking. He hugged me hard. Eventually my heart rate got back to normal. I even got back up there and mowed a bit. Pressing the clutch disengages the drive train and makes the tractor stop immediately. It's even more effective than pressing the brake pedal. I like to think of it as similar to praying. When we're running into trouble with our minds going crazy or immersed in some sin, we can just pray. Simply cry out to Jesus. It disengages the motor of our runaway mind, our emotions, and stops us in our tracks so we can stand in the presence of God and be safe and sane again in His love.

I also came to realize that all the risks my husband took were calculated. In his weird way, Casey was careful. He never did blow himself up. He just burned brighter as he got older. And like a bug, I was attracted to the light.

Chapter 24

Ecclesiastes 3:1–2 (KJV)

"To everything there is a season, and a time to every
purpose under the heaven: A time to be born, and
a time to die; a time to plant, and a time to pluck
up that which is planted."

IT WAS THE YEAR AFTER WE MOVED INTO
our little country place that Daddy died. Over the years, he and
Cecilia had grown close. She was with him at the end. When our
daughter called us with the news, Casey and I dropped everything
to make the trek to Texas. Now in her eighties, June was grateful to
have Cecilia there, who basically took charge of the arrangements. A
stay-at-home mom, Cecilia had left her husband and two kids back
here in Florida. Cecilia's husband, Kent, owned a large air conditioning company and had flown us and Mom to Texas in his own jet.
Marcus and his wife and three kids drove, arriving the day after us.

It was a big deal. Daddy had a lot of friends and associates, plus
he and June were involved in a number of charities after his retirement. I'd say there were well over a hundred at the grave site amid an
abundance of bouquets. Naturally, I wanted to know if Daddy was
saved before he passed. Cecilia, understanding me so well, assured
me of that right off the bat before I even got to ask.

"June and I prayed with him before he lost consciousness, Mom,"
she explained at our arrival. "Grandpa smiled and said he'd already

taken care of business with the Lord and not to worry. He squeezed both our hands and said he'd see us in Heaven. Oh, and he wanted you to know that he's really proud of you, Mom."

Wow, Father God. Thank you!

The memorial service was unforgettable. Is that redundant? Anyway, there was a bag piper, a small choir from an orphanage, and a color guard from the local police benevolent society to honor him. Cecilia rented the Good Fellow's lodge for a catered reception that served all those people. Two pastors spoke, a video screen reviewed his full life, and several community leaders gave short eulogies. At June's request, Cecilia seated Mom next to June, which I thought was awfully nice. Mom didn't expect to be honored like that, and it really moved her. Afterward, Cecilia and her kids stayed with June for a couple of weeks to ease her adjustment to widowhood. Our daughter thought of everything and conducted the whole affair with grace and dignity. As Daddy said so long ago about Cecilia, she's something else.

Back on the home scene, Marcus had been on a treasure hunt, anticipating his dad's sixtieth birthday. Keeping a secret from Casey was not easy, especially when a number of people in the antique auto world got involved. But somehow or other, Marcus pulled it off. It took over a year of tireless investigation, but he finally found the prize at a substantial cost.

Concealing it became the next challenge. Marcus and Marcie bought a place on the West side of town in a fancy planned community that catered to professionals like him. Their three-car garage was where the surprise was hidden. Whenever Casey visited their place, he'd poke around the garage to see what, if any, new toys his kid had. Marcus may have made a living, doctoring people's teeth, but he had his share of motor oil in his blood, too. So when we all gathered at Marcus and Marcie's for Thanksgiving, he almost had to physically stop Casey from wandering into the garage to admire a classic Harley touring bike, which was parked next to the birthday gift. No way was Marcus going to let Casey spoil the hard-won surprise. No doubt, my husband had a motorcycle ride on his mind.

Praise the Lord, it was raining that day and not too terribly diffi-cult to deter him. Plus, I distracted my sweet-toothed darling with pecan pie.

Christmas rolled by, and January brought in the usual clear, cool weather we Floridians find so refreshing. January was also when we celebrated Casey's birthday out at our place with a huge cookout. Sheila and Paul's family, Pastor Rick and Donna, many other friends, neighbors, trike club members, customers and employees, Casey's sister, of course my mom, plus dear June from Texas, all came to love on good old Casey as he embarked upon another decade of life.

Nearly everyone was there, when Casey asked Cecilia where Marcus's family was. That's when she told him that Marcus was coming with a special present, which we knew was just down the road. Cecilia asked her dad to sit down and wait.

A couple minutes later, Casey heard it before he saw it. There's something distinctly thrilling about the roar of Flow Masters in a 1972 Oldsmobile Cutlass Supreme with a 442 engine. As the sleek beauty tilted onto the driveway, Casey lurched up, knocking the folding chair back, with hands straight up and jaw dropped down. Marcus floored it, causing his wife riding shotgun and the kids in the back seat to scream. Sailing along with its rag top lowered, the chrome and jet-black muscle car (the very one that Casey and his dad had restored in his youth) dramatically vroomed with all eight cylinders pounding perfectly up to my husband and skid to a halt. Casey laid his hands on the long hood, still vibrating magnificently like a proud Motown thoroughbred, and grinned, teary-eyed, at his beaming son.

It was a perfect day for an outdoor party, and folks did what we'd hoped. They tarried. As the shadows lengthened, Paul tuned his guitar by the lit fire pit. We gathered around the crackling warmth. Even the trikers joined in on some of the more popular hymns, like "Amazing Grace." We sang "God Bless America" as the sun lit the western sky in shades of purple and peach.

Casey put his arm around me on the swing chair and tickled my ear with his breath. "Wanta go for a ride, Red?"

I could've swooned. Here I was, 61 years old, and this man made me feel like 16.

The Cutlass was a lot noisier than the trike. We didn't talk much. I'd slipped into my old blue jean jacket and slid down in the bucket seat as Casey wheeled Black Beauty down the driveway and onto our quiet two-lane county road. A flock of ibis flew overhead, their white feathers reflecting the pink glow of sunset. I gazed at the beloved profile of my masculine man and saw pleasure personified. I was so happy that he was so happy. More in love than ever, I wanted this ride to last forever.

Eyes glittering, Casey looked over at me looking at him. He squeezed my leg and nodded. He understood. Casey always seemed to understand me. Even back on campus when he witnessed my confrontation so long ago with Stuart, he saw me clearly. It was as if the Holy Spirit had tuned this man to my frequency and eventually, the Lord graciously tuned me to this man. I may have been a little slow to get it sometimes, but I eventually caught up. You'll see what I mean about that, too. And sooner than I would have chosen.

Chapter 25

Revelation 3:20 (NIV)

"Here I am! I stand at the door and knock. If anyone
hears My voice and opens the door, I will come in
and eat with that person, and they with Me."

IT'S A FUNNY THING, GETTING UP THERE
in years. I'd look in the mirror and hardly recognize myself. I hope
this makes sense to you, but, according to my self-image, it felt like
I was still in my 20s. Of course, I knew I'd changed a lot over the
years, and not just physically. My language had mellowed along with
my temperament. I was more grateful, less restless, and much more
patient. Retiring at 65, I began to draw Social Security. The following year, Casey planned to do the same. He'd changed, too, not
so much physically (except for maybe 20 or 30 extra pounds), but
I think his outlook shifted. Or maybe I should say his inlook. He
spent a lot more time in prayer and reading his Bible, which was
full of notes. Casey's spiritual progress was evidenced in an uncanny
knowing of things he would ordinarily not know. I attributed this
to his close walk with the Holy Spirit. My admiration for my husband grew as I witnessed this inside track he had with God, which
you will soon understand.

Anyway, we were taking steps to sell the business. Remember
Cody, the one who caused the EPA to fine us? He was married by
then, ran the shop excellently, and wanted to buy us out. I can assure

you that Casey had learned to completely trust him after the kid learned his lesson over the EPA incident.

This left Casey with more time on his hands and less involvement in worldly business. He still helped folks out with repairs and tractor stuff, plus he tinkered with Black Beauty, which had the propensity to require frequent tweaking. We alternated sunset drives in the convertible and on Red's Ride. Except for special events and holidays, we saw less of the kids, who were busy with their own kids and careers. Nevertheless, we felt well connected to them at heart and spoke or texted frequently.

I was no longer involved at the church school. I'd taken up gardening and continued with my painting. Every morning, we'd pray with Mom. She had a little lap dog she'd walk and watch Christian TV and occasionally a game show with. Things were slow-waltzing along when tragedy struck. Mom fell.

Somehow, little Prissy got under foot on a potty walk. I heard Mom scream in pain and ran over, tearing off gardening gloves and fumbling for the phone in my back pocket. Casey heard the commotion, ran out of the home shop, quickly assessed the need for an ambulance, and grabbed that phone out of my trembling hands.

Healthy at age 85, the doctors assured us that Mom had a very good chance of a full recovery from her broken hip. Sure enough, the hip replacement surgery went well. She was days away from being discharged from the nursing home, having completed their in-house physical therapy and mastery of a walker, when tragedy struck again—MRSA.

MRSA is a rabid staph infection. Mom suddenly complained about a soreness around the incision site. Within 24 hours, a full-blown invasion had driven down her leg and into her groin. She was immediately sent back into emergency surgery. This time things did not go well. I don't know why, but I suspect that the extremely strong IV antibiotics, although necessary, as well as the infection entering into her blood stream, simply sapped her physical strength. She asked to go home.

The day we packed her hospital room up, two nurses and an orderly were present to say goodbye and get her settled in her new wheelchair. They'd all learned to love her humor and spunk, plus she made a point of praying for everyone and their families.

As Casey was about to push her into the hall, Mom warned us, "I want you two to keep my bedroom door open at home." Then she shook her finger at Casey and exclaimed, "And that's not an invitation!"

The staff roared with laughter.

Evidently, Mom's filter had been slightly affected by the pain-killers. Anyway, Casey was a good sport, chuckled and consented to honor her hilariously unnecessary prohibition.

It wasn't easy to see Mom going downhill. But she didn't seem to mind at all. She was pleasantly compliant and happy to be home. We'd set up a hospital bed and potty chair in her room. At this point she was so weak that she needed help with everything, so I got a crash course in primary care.

As I wheeled her into the freshly adapted room upon her arrival, Casey had a proclamation of his own. "I'll help any way I can. But I do not want to see her naked, and I won't deal with poop!"

I set Mom on the edge of the bed next to a nice clean nighty and undressed her that first evening. She said she had to poop. So I positioned myself to transfer her to the potty chair right next to the bed, when she went dead weight on me, slow motion slipped through my arms and slid her naked self on the floor, where she promptly pooped.

I screamed, "*Casey!*"

He burst into the room to be greeted by his worst nightmare. So much for proclamations.

Anyway, he gently scooped her up and eased her back to the bed where I spent the next hour cleaning her, the floor, the bed, and myself. Welcome home, Mom!

Every day was a tender reminder of the fragility of these earth suits we so cavalierly take for granted. Mom didn't care to eat. Just getting liquids into her was a chore. Still, she wanted to watch her favorite preachers on TV and outguess the *Wheel of Fortune* contestants. And of course, she cuddled with Prissy, who was beyond joy to have her mistress back. As inseparable as they were, one of my favorite pictures from this time is of the little imp perched on Mom's lap after having had some minor surgery, herself, which required that annoying doggie plastic bell. No mutt ever looked cuter as a cone head. When I attempted to give them each their medication, I got the exact same expression: chin up, eyes squeezed shut, and lips tightly pinched. They even both shook their heads in tandem, making that mmmm hmmmm "*No!*" sound.

About a week into Mom's homecoming, Casey and I were awakened by her crying. He flung the covers back, swung those long legs off the bed, and marched into her room, muttering, "That does it."

This wasn't the first time she whimpered in her sleep. Since the second surgery, Mom had had fearsome nightmares.

My warrior husband briefly stood at attention as she wrestled with the unseen and then he let it rip, roaring, "You devil, I command you to go in the power of Jesus's name!" He came back to bed dusting his hands. "That oughta do it," he stated, and slept soundly as I waited and heard nothing but peaceful silence.

Mom slept a solid 12 hours.

Memorial Day approached, and along with it came a thunderstorm, which brought a big tree down on our neighbor's roof. Casey grabbed his chain saw, and we both went over there to help with the clean-up and tarping. Sheila came over and sat with Mom while we were gone.

The next day was the holiday, and I did everything I knew to make Mom happy and comfortable. I massaged her with lotion. I read to her out of her Bible. I wheeled her and Prissy onto the front porch where Mom was non-verbal but smiling contentedly at the hummingbird and butterflies drinking honey suckle nectar. It got muggy, so I brought her in. I asked if she was in any pain. She shook her head no and smiled. I went into the kitchen to prepare electrolytes for her and Prissy when Casey came barreling into the house from the shop.

"Put that down!" he barked at me as he ran over to Mom. "Get over here, Marney, and pray." As soon as he said, "Jesus," she was gone. Just like that. Not a whimper, just a sweet smile, a last little breath, and boof! Gone!

After 911, you know who I called. Sheila rushed over immediately. She and Paul, the kids, the neighbors, all kinds of people eventually came. Furniture got rearranged. Plans got quickly enacted. A beautiful memorial took place. I basically dream-walked through the whole thing. I was exhausted. The ordeal of being on point ever since her first fall and then the intense care at home for two weeks left me almost numb. I cried a lot. But they were mostly tears of gratitude. Mom went home to Jesus. She was a good mother, after all. This serene ending of her lifetime outweighed all the crap that came before.

The last thing I read to Mom out of her Bible was Hosea 6:3 (KJV) "Then shall we know, if we follow on to know the Lord: His going forth is prepared as the morning; and He shall come unto us as the rain, as the latter and former rain unto the earth." I have it marked in her Bible, along with the date of Mom's departure. We may start out rough, but what matters is how we finish. As the Apostle Paul said in Hebrews 3:6 (KJV) "But Christ as a son over his own house; whose house are we, if we hold fast the confidence and the rejoicing of the hope firm unto the end."

I thanked God for the refreshing, joyous latter rain at the conclusion of my mother's life here on Earth.

I tried befriending poor, sad little Prissy, but she wouldn't have me, as if it was my fault. She just lay in the corner where Mom's recliner used to be and whined. One day, I got a call from an elderly lady at our church whose dog had died. She heard that we were giving a wee lap mutt away. I told her to come over. It was instant love. As this sweet little lady and her husband drove away with Prissy, I heaved a sigh and prayed, "Ah Lord, You give and You take away. You do all things well, and I praise You."

Chapter 26

Daniel 2:22 (NIV)

"He reveals deep and hidden things; He knows what lies in darkness, and light dwells with Him."

AS I MENTIONED BEFORE, CASEY POR-trayed a remarkable gift. He heard from God. Of course, every born-again follower of Jesus Christ has access to this. Salvation through Christ is just the beginning. There's much more. As Jesus said to His followers, He'd send the Holy Spirit to them after ascending to His Father in Heaven. This is the same Holy Spirit that Jesus listened to when He walked the earth as a man and by Whose power Jesus performed many miracles. The indwelling Holy Spirit, the third person of the Godhead, brings incredible abilities, including supernatural wisdom and knowledge.

Whenever Casey got a Holy Ghost download, he didn't brag about it. He'd just do amazing stuff because he knew what was about to happen. Obviously, this included Mom's imminent passing. He charged to her side, all dirty from messing around in the shop, to pray her off to eternity. Now, how else could he have known that?

Well, this happening became more and more frequent. For example, one day he told me to fix extra for dinner. Sure enough, Marcus and his brood showed up with a new boat and a surprise plan to take us fishing the next morning. We had a blast at a local lake, plus they joined us at church that weekend before heading back to their new home in Tallahassee.

Another time, Casey unexpectedly veered off our normal route as we returned home from our sunset ride. There, down a dirt road, were a cow and a bull enjoying clover on the shoulder. Casey drove up to the farmhouse to let them know and then proceeded to coax the cattle back to the broken gate with the trike. That led to a conversation with the farmer about, you guessed it, Jesus. We prayed with the young man for the Lord to ignite his spirit and prosper the work of his hands. We got home in the dark, but Casey left a generous deposit of Holy fire at the farm.

All this impressed me tremendously, as you can imagine. I began to rely more and more on my husband's spiritual leadership and the strength of his faith. I'd let him and others know it, too. As much earlier in our journey together, he'd detect this adoration as a problem and warn, "Cut it out, Marney. You're gunna get me in trouble."

As Casey's sixty-fifth birthday approached, he seemed a little detached. He'd accomplished pretty much what he wanted materially. He had no desire to travel. He'd built stuff, invented a few things, acquired all the tools any Mr. Fixit could ever desire, plus he'd had the joy of seeing his children and grandchildren grow and prosper. Then, one morning, he surged out the door after breakfast with a double dose of his old enthusiasm. I brought a glass of sweet tea out to the shop later on and found him on his knees whacking at the gears of a car lift.

"What are you doin', Honey?" I asked.

He reached up for the sweating tumbler. "Just servicing this thing. It's been sticking" He set the glass down on the cement floor and picked up a grease gun.

I walked back into the house to pay a few bills and make lunch. By 1:30 he still hadn't come in. I found him under the hood of the tractor, cleaning the air filter. By the end of the day, he had also thoroughly serviced the truck, the car, the trike, the air compressor, two welders, and the lawn mower.

I called him in for dinner. As I looked out the kitchen window, I saw him spraying the little screened gazebo he built in the yard.

"Casey! What are you doing?"

"Just waterproofing your gazebo, Red. I'm using automotive clear so it'll last," he explained, and continued to cover the wooden love seat swing he built into it, while whistling to the tune of "Blessed Redeemer, Jesus is Mine."

The words, "Oh what a foretaste of glory divine," echoed in my head as he finally came in and headed for the shower. After dinner, he asked if I wanted to go for a ride. I climbed onto the trike and he backed it out of the garage. He put on our favorite CD of Michael W Smith's praise music, and we cruised into the sunset. It was late, so we did the short ride. Cresting the hill on the way home under fading orange and purple and a blushing half-moon, we sang the last "Amen" of "Revelation Song."

I was tired, and my back hurt. I told Casey I had to lie down. He responded with a grin and an offer. "You wanta a massage, Red?"

Now, this was out of character. I mean, for this man to suddenly work all day like a manic grease monkey after a period of placidity was weird enough. But Casey, in all our years together, had *never* offered to give me a back rub. Sure, I'd asked and he'd responded with the obligatory husband-style rub rub, squeeze squeeze, and then done. This time, I got a real massage and was totally relaxed, all back pain melted away under his strong fingers.

Then, without a howdy doo, he flipped me over, made love to me, and, suddenly, his face inches from mine, his mouth burst into a glowing beam and his eyes bulged open wide as if he was seeing someone or something beyond amazing. A heartbeat later, he simply went away.

"Casey?' Something was wrong.

"*Casey!*" I screamed as he slowly, effortlessly rolled off me and emitted a rattled snore. The eyes that I had adoringly gazed into seconds ago were vacant.

"Casey, this isn't funny!" I sobbed as I began chest compressions and fumbled for the phone on the nightstand.

It was while the 911 operator coached me that I realized this might be a great time to pray. I set the phone down on the pillow and cried almost mindlessly, "Jesus, Jesus, help me, Jesus!"

The fire rescue people worked on him for 10 minutes. They got nothing. I called Marcus, Cecilia, and Sheila. The sheriff came and asked too many questions while four big EMTs hefted him off the bed and onto a gurney. They wouldn't let me in the ambulance. I nervously drove behind it. Why were they going so slow?" Why didn't they have their siren on? Wasn't this an emergency? Being closer to town, Sheila and Paul were already at the ER when we got there. Paul wrapped us both in his arms as the waiting room speakers announced, "Code Blue," sending a chill through my bones. Minutes later, Cecilia and her husband arrived. We were all ushered into a little conference room. The doctor came in within minutes to apologetically express his sympathy. Marcus and Marcie arrived three hours later. We all stood hand-in-hand around Casey's body in a stark, back room.

Marcus said, "Let's do what Dad would do. Let's believe in a miracle."

We held hands, prayed, and called for him to rise from the dead. But Casey didn't want to. I knew it even before we started. Please don't chastise me for unbelief. I wanted with all my being for him to come back. But I'd seen his eyes glow with joy upon being greeted by an angel or whatever it was that he saw. I knew he would never come back, no matter how hard we prayed. Casey was home and happy.

Chapter 27

Hebrews 4:14–15 (NIV)

"Therefore, since we have a great high priest Who has ascended into heaven, Jesus the Son of God, let us hold firmly to the faith we profess. For we do not have a high priest who is unable to empathize with our weaknesses, but we have one who has been tempted in every way, just as we are—yet He did not sin.

SHEILA AND PAUL CONSULTED WITH the kids and arranged for a wonderful church service and reception back at our place (now just my place). They pulled Red's Ride and Black Beauty out into the big side yard to flank a display of pictures highlighting a life fully lived. It was a beautiful fall day. The air was finally brisk after the long, hot summer. Our (I mean my) water maples and decorative pear trees had turned burnished red. Pink and red camellias were blossoming early, and even a few gardenia bushes displayed fragrant white flowers that day. Paul had fired up the big smoker that Casey had built out of a propane tank. Chairs and tables accommodated well over a hundred people who enjoyed the Southern style barbeque Casey used to scarf down.

An open mic allowed everyone to step up and honor the man they'd loved and admired. I heard stories of Casey's generosity I never knew before. As the day went on, more neighbors, including the farmer family with the wayward cow and bull, came to tell of how a good Christian man like Casey could make an enormous difference. A single mother whose son Casey had befriended said, "You never know what just a smile can do." Our pastor really surprised me. He choked out, "I don't have any words, for a change, except to say, Casey McKay was my friend." He sat back down, hands folded. The elderly couple next door worriedly wondered who was going to help them out whenever they had an emergency.

Ha! *They* wondered? What about *me*?

Despite my pain and turmoil, I smiled, hugged, kissed, thanked, laughed at Casey jokes, and appeared altogether. No one knew how phony I was. Except for God. And Sheila. She let others do the serving. She just stuck close to me. No talking needed this time from Sheila. Just being there quiet and easy amid the swirl.

I didn't tell you this before, but when Casey and I'd prayed together that morning (as we did every morning), he asked, "Is this the day I get to meet you, Jesus?"

That right there should have been my clue. He knew it! Why didn't he tell me? He just serviced, well, everything, myself included.

I was steamed. I was also brokenhearted and scared witless.

My emotions whirled in a blender as I internally careened toward the cliff of despair. The solid life I thought I had just crumbled and disappeared. I was free falling with no ground to stand on. I didn't know who I was without my husband. Had I returned to the starting line all over again, searching for my identity? Where was God in this?

After the people left, I brought Marcus into our little home office. Casey's urn sat on the desk. I pointed him to it and tried to explain that I just couldn't deal with it. I didn't say this to our son, but I liked Casey's body a whole lot the way it was and the contents of that jar were repugnant to me. He looked at it for a moment, picked it up, gave me a firm one-armed hug and kissed the top of my head, as if I was the child. Then he looked down again at the desk and whispered past the lump in his throat, "Is that Dad's Bible?"

I said it was. He swooped it up in his other hand and walked out, eyes wet and jaw set, looking so much like his father. I sat down on the desk chair, stared at the Bible's spot just vacated before me, laid my head down, and sobbed. The day he died, the last verse Casey had read in that book was where the Apostle Paul was about to leave this mortal world. Corinthians II 5:8 (KJV) "We are confident, I say, and willing rather to be absent from the body, and to be present with the Lord."

I didn't go to church the next day. I didn't get dressed. I didn't have breakfast. Sheila found me sitting out in the gazebo, just staring at nothing.

"How was church?" I pretended interest as she sat opposite me.

"Pastor had Casey's picture up on the screen, and we all prayed for you." She smiled tenderly as I finally made eye contact.

I tried to take a deep breath and scolded myself for not being there.

"Don't blame yourself, Marney," she addressed my silent suffering.

Without another word, my sweet friend just slipped down in front of me on her knees and held out her arms. I slid into them and let her love me as we both cried on the floor of the little screened room where Casey and I used to swing side-by-side under the stars.

About three weeks later, after continual moping and going through the motions of living, I got sick of sorrow and whining. Why had he died? Why didn't we know he had a heart condition? How am I going to manage without him?

I halfheartedly thumbed through my Bible, set it down, and pushed to the edge of the couch.

Suddenly, I let God have it.

I shook my fist at the ceiling. "Oh, *fine*, Jesus!" I shouted. "You and Casey are up there. What about me?"

I stood up, panting, and shaking, fists clenched in defiance.

"Sit down, My Precious One," I distinctly heard vibrate within my raging chest.

Momentarily chastened, I plopped back down on the cushion.

"I've always taken care of you."

Swelling love waves released the anger from my heart. But I couldn't take the Lord's mercy in completely. Not right away. My ego resisted. I briefly allowed grief to swamp me again. But the wailing seemed somehow phony, forced. So I took a good look at what was happening to me. I was wallowing in self-pity! Why would I want to choose this for myself? This was not life!

I shuddered at a mental picture of myself mired in sucking clay, unable to get out. That is, until I replayed the words just given by grace. "I've always taken care of you." And that's when I made a decision. I was going to trust God. Hadn't He always been faithful? If I had to start all over again, so be it. But I was not going to toss all the good stuff Jesus had poured into me. I was going to tell my mind to shut up and quit cursing myself. I would listen to the Holy Spirit, Who was patiently waiting for me to pay attention to Him.

"Just rest in Me," He crooned softly within my wounded spirit.

The writer of the Book of Hebrews said that we have to labor to enter into the Lord's rest. Believe me, it's work to do that. We have to take control of our thoughts and emotions. We have to tell ourselves that God promised good things to those who believe Him. We have to obey Him. He said to rejoice in all circumstances. Crazy as that sounds, it works. It's not easy, but it does get better with practice.

Being with God means letting His presence overwhelm us with perfect peace. The Sabbath is the day that the Jewish people, under the Law of Moses, were supposed to cease from all work and just spend time with their God, in prayer, meditation, and worship, and simply be with Him. Jesus is now our Sabbath rest. Or, like I heard a preacher on TV say, "When we work, God rests. When we rest, God works."

I let God go to work. I put on worship music and sang along. First off, I realized that asking "why" was, for me at this point, a poison question. If God wanted to show me why Casey left me, He'd do it at the perfect time, which you'll see.

I whirled around the living room to the music. I steered my soul under the power of the Holy spirit to turn self-pity into gratitude. I thanked the Lord for the many wonderful years I had with the man of my dreams. I thanked him for our children, grandchildren, and dear friends in Christ. I thanked Him for saving me from Hell. I thanked Him that, one day, I would be in Heaven and see King Jesus face-to-face. And I'd see Casey again, not as my husband, but as co-lover of the Lord, serving and worshipping in spiritual, glorified bodies with all the saints and Heavenly Host.

Cecilia popped in and discovered me swooping and flowing around the room in divinely inspired dance. I didn't hear her because I had the music so loud. She stood there with her hands to her cheeks in amazement. Tears streamed onto her fingertips. I turned to see her and stopped.

"Don't stop, Mom," she sobbed. "I feel the presence of the Holy Spirit. I think He's healing you."

Sure thing, my Jesus, Who gave me His precious Spirit, understood my grief and urgent need to be back in unity with the Father. He experienced all that and much more on the cross.

I took her hands in mine and lifted them. We swayed face-to-face. "He's healing us both, dear," I smiled.

We danced.

Chapter 28

Matthew 13:45–46 (NIV)

"Again, the kingdom of heaven is like a merchant
looking for fine pearls. When he found one of great
value, he went away and sold everything he had and
bought it."

DAYS TURNED TO WEEKS AND SO ON.
Christmas came and went, a muted but sweet remembrance of why
we celebrate this season. I thought that Marcus seemed remote. I
asked him if he'd done anything with his father's ashes. He mumbled that he hadn't decided what to do yet.

Winter gave way to spring and I earnestly wanted to set my
heart on things above, as Paul told the Colossian church in the
third chapter of that Bible book. But earthly things kept me distracted. I decided to keep the tractor, but a lot of other stuff had
to go. I divided the guns between the kids and kept one pistol. The
energy producing contraptions had me completely flummoxed. I'd
have to sort that out later. Marcus said he'd take Black Beauty off my
hands. That was a relief, as an antique auto requires much mainte-
nance. Plus, that loud muscle car only reminded me of the missing
driver who would never again blast it into warp speed, downshifting
like a NASCAR pro.

One special remaining relic had me stumped. I asked everyone in the family and several dear friends, but no one wanted Red's Ride. Not even Paul, for goodness sake.

As I watched him work, the guy who delivers propane to our (I mean my) house, made a suggestion. While the tank filled, I'd told him about Casey's passing. The friendly driver's shocked sadness turned to curiosity. Casey had always chatted and prayed with him with his typical warmth, and they shared a love for motorized vehicles of all sorts, so he was familiar with the trike.

He blurted, "Marney, why don't you drive that crazy motorcycle Casey made? You ought to enjoy it, you know? He would've liked that."

This was not the first person to urge me to use it. I was really trying to be open-minded about seeking God's will in my life, and I sure didn't want to sit around doing nothing. Being a widow was still an unfamiliar identity, and I knew I needed a fresh perspective. At this point, I'd decided not to turn down any decent invitation or idea. That's why I'd signed up for square dancing, joined the community church choir, and faithfully attended a ladies' home Bible study.

And that's why I signed up for the motorcycle driving course to get my endorsement. In Florida, you need to get that stamped on your driver's license. Now, Casey had taught me drive it, but I'd only gone around the yard a few times. With the automatic transmission from the Saturn, all I had to do was put my foot on the brake, shift it into drive just like a car, and idle forward. Steering was a bit tricky, and turns had to be taken wide. Remember, it had the Nissan's rear end, giving it a big fanny. A twist of the right handlebar, and it would accelerate suddenly.

I showed up at 8:00 a.m. sharp for the first class. I was the oldest person there. The other dozen students were, well, mostly college students, plus there was one middle-aged bona fide biker chick. The instructor, a retired motorcycle cop named Buck, looked us up and down, then assigned each one to an appropriately sized motorcycle supplied by the school.

He came to me last, scratched his beard, spit, and growled, "I'm gunna put you on a scooter." He emphasized the word, so it sounded like, "scooooter."

I'd never driven one and probably looked worried.

"You won't have to shift it," he explained, and proceeded to direct his assistant to unload a bright pink little scooter from their trailer.

The first lesson was easy. Turn it on, straddle it with both feet still on the ground, and just shuffle-walk with it.

Next, we sat on our bikes, the others shifted, we all gave them a bit of gas, and drove a short distance in a straight line, practicing stopping, and then going and stopping again. Not too bad.

By the end of the day, all the other students were turning, accelerating, shifting, and doing really well. I was always at the end of the line. On the last turn of the course that first day, I accelerated a bit too much. Buck flapped his arms, hollering, "Slow down, Grandma!"

I squeezed the lever on the handlebar that only operated the front wheel brake. The front of the scooter stopped as the still powered rear wheel surged, swinging to the left and bucked me right off.

Buck sauntered over to me after his assistant had already checked out potential wreckage. The bike was fine. I'd hit my head and wrenched my wrist. Thank the Lord Buck was a stickler on safety equipment. The helmet no doubt saved my noggin, and the glove from worse damage to my hand.

"You okay, Granny?" he rumbled.

"I'm fine," I squeaked.

He gave me that "I don't believe you" cop look, clapped his hands, and said we were done for the day.

That night I iced my wrist and found an old ace bandage in the bottom of a drawer. When I showed up the next morning, Becky the biker chick, noticed that I had the bandage on wrong. As she rewrapped me, Buck strode over to us, frowned, and asked if I was sure I wanted to continue. I said yes. Becky hugged me, and we mounted up.

Each course we drove racked up points if we made mistakes. The more mistakes, the more points. If you got 20 points, you failed.

By the end of the third and last day, I'd accumulated 19 points. If I hadn't passed the written part with a perfect score, I wouldn't have gotten my motorcycle endorsement.

At the end of the last class, Buck passed out our certificates of course completion. He extended mine to me last. As I took hold of the paper, he didn't let go. We locked eyes.

"Don't worry," I offered. "I'll never get on the interstate, and I'm only going to drive the trike my husband built."

I'd shown him a picture of Red's Ride. He said something that sounded like, "Hrmff," and released the certificate into my hand.

Later that day, I walked into the garage, stared at Red's Ride for a long time, turned around, walked out, and closed the door. I called the square dance instructor and thanked him for his humorous dance calls, offered to donate the fancy crinoline twirly skirts to the group, and quit. I picked up my Bible and searched for treasure that would not rust or turn to dust. I found it in the fourth chapter of Philippians 4:19 (KJV) "But my God shall supply all your need according to His riches in glory by Christ Jesus."

I knew what I needed, and it wasn't maniacally pursuing every activity possible or trying to relive the past. What I needed was to know and serve the God Who loved me. I needed to work my own faith to discover my spiritual purpose.

So I just held onto Him through the business of living in this world. I continued with the Bible study, church, and family. But instead of adding on useless busyness, I spent a lot more time in private worship and prayer. That screened gazebo, where Casey and I spent sweet time together at the end of day, became my prayer closet. I bought a plastic chair and faced it toward the sunrise. Next to it was a plastic table for my Bible and a notebook. I lifted my face to Heaven, opened my heart, and glorified the Lord with the kind of love that flows out of a deep well springing up in rapturous joy from my spirit. This became my new routine. Sometimes God would lead me to a scripture verse that would speak to me. Sometimes His message came from within, where His spirit lives in my spirit. The notebook began to fill with His love letters. These started out as encouragement and soon included specific instructions.

I was hearing from God! Oh, what a delight! Whenever I asked to hear from Him, He was ready with His words of truth and life. Plus, I had the words recorded in a notebook to review. One day, He told me to sell Red's Ride. He further explained that it was meant to be a blessing to another retired couple. I pulled it out by the road with a "for sale" sign. That day, a man called me. He said he'd never been down my road before and saw that trike. Could he come by and check it out?

Following God's script, this retired Army veteran drove it around a bit and explained that he was looking for something he and his wife could do together. They had recently lost their son to a drug overdose. I listened to his story with a full heart. The idea of having this unique machine to carry and console his sweetheart gave an aging warrior hope. The next day, his wife and he came back with the cash. They were about to observe their fortieth wedding anniversary, but they didn't much feel like celebrating. I told them about Casey. We held hands, and I prayed for their healing journey ahead.

It was almost sunset when they drove away, she in the car and he on the trike. I walked back into the garage with the aim of sorting through all the junk I cleaned out of the side compartments and trunk. I picked up the CD we used to listen to, and it hit me like a hammer. Never would I ride behind those broad shoulders again singing as the sun set. I sunk to my knees and wailed. Convulsing sobs erupted until I couldn't catch my breath. And then I felt Him. His gracious love enveloped me. He knew how I felt. The comfort of God is not just a little "There, there, you'll be all right." It's actual compassion. Jesus didn't just know my sorrow, He shared it.

Jesus is my treasure, the best friend you could ever imagine. It surprised me, this slam of grief. I thought I was getting over it. But just so you know, whenever you lose someone you love, it's a winding road. A song, a picture, a smell, a card, any old thing can suddenly take you back. But keep heart. Embrace the moment, but don't cling to it too long. Don't make that the sum of your life. If you know the Lord (and I hope you do), grab onto Him. He sure won't lose His hold of you. The realization of His tender presence floods you with a love that never fails. The strength I gained from realizing this helped me in the challenges yet to come.

Chapter 29

Philippians 1:4–6 (NIV)

"In all my prayers for all of you, I always pray with
joy because of your partnership in the gospel from
the first day until now, being confident of this, that
He Who began a good work in you will carry it on
to completion until the day of Christ Jesus."

"I DECIDED WHAT TO DO WITH DAD'S
ashes."

This was the best Marcus had sounded in weeks. "That's great,
Marcus." I hesitated to ask what it was.

"I'm going to take him fishing." He finished the thought with
enthusiasm.

Already, my mind went to wind direction when I asked, "Where?"

"We're going to launch from the Suwannee near Manatee
Springs and sail out into the Gulf," he explained. "You're coming
with us, aren't you?"

"Uh, well, sure," I said. "Who all's coming?"

"Just Marcie and I, Cecilia and Kent and you. No kids. Oh, and
do you think that Sheila and Paul would like to come?"

Right away, I knew that I needed Sheila to be there. I told
Marcus I'd call her, and we decided to settle on a date as soon as
everyone had a day free. Sheila called me back that afternoon and
suggested we do it on Memorial Day. By evening, our plan was

set. We'd meet at the boat launch next Monday morning with a lunch and our hearts prepared for whatever ceremony Marcus had in mind. Honestly, I wasn't too crazy about doing this at first, but the more I thought about it, the better I felt. I knew that Casey was in Heaven with Jesus. I knew that Sheila would be there, offering her usual gentle strength. I was feeling stronger, closer to the Lord with my own reliance on His grace. Not only could I do this, but I was determined to be positively present for our children. After all, Cecilia and Marcus were grieving the loss of their wonderful father. I needed to be strong for our kids.

By the time Marcus got us out into the open waters of the Gulf of Mexico, it was midday and getting hot. I plunked myself down on a seat under the Bimini top and enjoyed the expansive blue ocean and sky. We continued westward for several miles under fluffy cumulus clouds. A pleasant breeze produced by the boat's motion refreshed us, and the rhythmic slap of waves against the hull lulled us into serenity. We ate our picnic lunch. There was little conversation, just an easy comradery tinged with purpose.

Finally, Marcus dropped the anchor. The boat swiveled around to the north and then faced east. No shoreline appeared, just diamond tipped little waves gently rolling landward. At her husband's nod, Marcie opened a small cooler and brought out a bottle of wine, little plastic cups, and a baggie of crackers.

"Looks like communion to me," Paul said. "What a great idea!"

"Yup, it came to me after I prayed a few weeks ago," Marcus replied. "I asked the Lord what to do with Dad's ashes. I heard Him say in my spirit, "Bring it to the cross.""

Cecilia picked up the story. "So that's when Marcus called me. He knew he had to bring, not just the ashes, but the whole thing, including the closure we needed to honor Dad, to the cross and the finished work of Jesus. What better way to remember what God has done for us than to break the bread and drink the cup just as Jesus instructed us to? Anyway, that's how we came up with this plan."

While Cecilia spoke, she looked at each of us for our reactions. She got warm smiles of understanding and approval as Marcie passed out the cups and crackers. Marcus continued to explain that the best way to honor a Christian's life is to remember what God did for him at Calvary, where the Lord laid down His own life for him. He invited each one of us to say something before we received the emblems of Jesus's body and blood.

My turn came last. "Dear Father God," I began, "You knew all along what it would take to get us back. It took sacrificing Your own dear Son. You put all your disgust and judgment for fallen humanity upon pure, innocent Jesus, and for a brief time, that separated the two of You. What agony You both suffered! But Jesus obeyed You for our sakes. His wounded head gives us a sound mind. His shredded skin and muscles heal our diseases. His bruises cover our gross selfishness. His broken body, represented by this broken bread, made a way to adopt us into Your family, Your body, the Church.

"But that wasn't enough for You, Heavenly Father. No! You allowed Jesus's precious blood to be sweated out in passionate prayer the night before. Then, on the cross, it flowed to the sad ground so that we could be fully redeemed for Your Kingdom. His blood, represented by the juice of crushed grapes, has sealed us into this great grace covenant that cannot be annulled.

"And even more than all this, Dear God, You arranged by Your Spirit for Jesus to resurrect and ascend to Heaven so that He could send wonderful Holy Spirit to dwell within us, giving us His presence and power to faithfully live for Your dear cause. And that's exactly what Casey's life exemplified. So we humbly honor You, God. We praise You for what You did for Casey. We examine ourselves and see Your amazing victory in each of our lives. We are alive in You forever! I and my loved ones today thank You, Lord Jesus, with our whole hearts for Your body and Your blood. You bought us with Love."

Dear friend, there's just something about observing the Lord's supper like this that catapults you into a deeper awareness of God's amazing grace. We ate the crackers and drank the wine with reverent awe. The sun behind us was inching toward the horizon. The wind died down completely. Other than the gentle lapping of waves, there was silence. Then, Casey reached into a bag, pulled out the urn, and walked to the stern. We quietly flanked him as he removed the stopper and tipped the contents to the still air and rolling sea. Somewhere, a gull cried. I felt those Holy Ghost shivers.

Sheila began to sing, "Amazing Grace, how sweet the sound, that saved a wretch like me."

One by one we all joined in, "I once was lost but now I'm found, was blind but now I see."

Another bird called. The wind picked up as our voices built. "How precious did that grace appear the hour I first believed."

Clouds began appearing near the horizon, quickly tumbling our way. Casey cranked the motor, and Paul brought up the anchor. We headed toward shore. I remained at the stern, watching pastel colors gather around the clouds: soft peach, pink, and lavender.

Before my son hit full throttle, we belted out, "When we've been there 10,000 years, bright shining as the sun, we've no less days to sing God's praise, than when we first begun."

The boat sped toward the mouth of the Suwannee with an increasing tail wind. Our mood raced, too. We felt the exuberance of wind and spay and pulsating life. The entire sunset sky strengthened gloriously, a dramatic dark purple dome tinged with gold all around us. On the river, the wind decreased. Intense celestial hues of royal blue with fire tipped cloud fingers waved us home. By the time we finally idled up to the boat ramp, it was almost full dark.

That night I dreamed. It started with me lying down in the hull of a small boat, perhaps a canoe. The water gently rocked me right and left, my shoulders and hips barely touching the sides. A soft spray misted down upon my face. I felt strangely relaxed and simultaneously alert. Then, my prone body started rising above the boat. Unseen arms cradled me as I rose into the sky. Gently swaying, securely but lightly held, I felt no fear of the increasing height. I sensed light beaming brightly upon my face but kept my eyes closed. Then, a warm, fragrant breath passed over me, and I heard, "This is how I love you. Depend on Me."

I woke with a start. The sun's first filtered light peeked through my bedroom window. I gasped, uncomprehending at first that I was alone. I thought I felt a presence. "Casey?" I whispered, afraid. Blinking more awake into the silence, I padded over to the window, which I'd left open. It was raining softly. A light wind invited the smell of freshness, and a neighbor's rooster crowed. I made a cup of coffee, picked up my Bible, and settled on the covered back porch. There I turned to this verse: John 15:5 (NIV) "I am the vine; you are the branches. If you remain in me and I in you, you will bear much fruit; apart from me you can do nothing."

What now? I wondered. I walked back into the kitchen and saw the half-full bottle of wine left over from Casey's last boat ride. I dribbled a small amount into a mug, broke off a pinch of bread crust, and went back to my porch chair. Holding the bread, I thanked Father God for sending Jesus to be broken, shredded, tormented for my wholeness and wellness and ate the crumb. I held the cup up and saluted Heaven for the final sacrifice God gave of Himself to wash me clean and cover me with His Son's righteousness.

"You can do more," that gentle voice intoned in my spirit.

I pondered what that could be and heard one more word: "Fight."

Propelled with a surge of warrior power, I began to pray. I prayed for abortion workers to get sick of the slaughter. I prayed for educators caught up in a rebellious spirit of false teaching. I prayed for children and college students, that they would vomit out the lies and cry to God for truth. I prayed for the churches that they would wake up, turn from minimizing the Bible, but teach the full Gospel of Jesus Christ and be ready to receive the lost. I prayed for the doors of hearts to open up to the Father's love. I prayed for the president, the congressional members, the courts, the state and local governments around the nation. I prayed for doctors and nurses, for law enforcement, first responders and military personnel. I prayed for wisdom, discernment and protection, for good government and brotherly love. I prayed for the peace of Jerusalem and that the Jewish people would come to the cross and receive their Messiah.

I cursed the curses of the evil one. I commanded by the authority given to me that his fiery darts would return to him. I proclaimed confusion in the enemy camp in the mighty name of Jesus. I prayed that the lost, hurting, confused, and depressed would turn their backs on the world and cry out to the Lord. I prayed that the wicked would become the righteous. I prayed that many cultists, witches, child molesters, pushers, and haters would come quickly to salvation in Jesus Christ.

I danced, weeping and rejoicing.

Chapter 30

2 Timothy 3:5–7 (KJV)

"Having a form of godliness, but denying the power thereof: from such turn away. For of this sort are they which creep into houses, and lead captive silly women laden with sins, led away with divers lusts, ever learning, and never able to come to the knowledge of the truth."

OVER A YEAR HAS PASSED SINCE WE TOOK my husband's ashes into the Gulf of Mexico. Since then, I've had the opportunity to host a couple of teenagers. They came by way of my church. One of them was pregnant and homeless and lived with me for six months. She is now the mother of twins, engaged to be married and has an apartment and a job. The other one just moved out yesterday. I helped her get her identity straightened out so she could get her GED. She starts community college next semester and will be rooming with a couple of other girls from her youth group. This one'd been trafficked since before puberty by her own "family." She's come a long way, thanks to a sexual healing course offered by the local Christian pregnancy center.

I often think of how I placed myself in harm's way when around their age. How I miraculously survived my own youth can simply be attributed to God's mercy. I guess He knew all along I'd somehow be joined to His Kingdom family and do a bit of service there. But mostly, I know it's simply because He loves me and wanted better for me, just as He does for these precious young women who are learning to trust and follow the Lord.

Feeling a little empty nest blues, I got together with Sheila for lunch and a little shopping. I needed a dress for their anniversary party coming up. Forty years my friends have been together, and their marriage is still going strong. As we drove to the mall, Sheila asked me if I had any insights into what God was doing with this nation. That surprised me. I had to really think about it. We'd been grousing some over the lack of civility in public debate. It used to be that we'd say to opponents, "I disagree with you, but I defend your right to your opinion." Now political correctness borders on censorship and even spills into violence. That really disturbs us both.

"It's all such a mess," I started. "But God brings some things into our lives to break us so He can make us trust Him more. Like, right now kids seem so disconnected to this nation's roots. They don't really know that this country was founded on biblical ethics, rules, and morals. And they seem so intolerant of free expression. Many actually think that socialism, Big Brother, is a good idea. But I have to believe that, at some point, they'll see the futility of expecting government to be their daddy.

Sheila agreed. "Evidently, youth today have suffered from broken families to such an extent that they don't know how to belong to a healthy society. Maybe it won't be too late for some of them to see the danger they face. I just hope they get sick of it all and cry out to God, instead of stifling freedom in their desperate need to feel security."

When she said that, I remembered how mistaken I'd been in my own youth. Better not judge, I warned myself. Be patient and loving.

"I was thinking about the one-world order thing," Sheila continued. "It seems like we're about to see the Book of Revelation manifesting right in our lifetime. But we aren't powerless. We may feel overwhelmed by current events, and yet we know that when we cry out to God, His power in us is perfected. Living in dependency on God is our strength and joy, despite the turmoil around us."

To my dismay, I had to purchase a dress a size larger than what I expected. Guess I need to lay off bread and desserts. Anyway, that night I finished an amazing book by Gwen Shaw entitled *Redeeming the Land*. In it, she explained the source of the Krishna movement I had gotten caught up in so long ago: Babylon. Yup, it goes all the way back in antiquity, a massive societal rebellion against God in ancient Babylon. You can also read about it in the Book of Genesis.

Satan is an imitator. He's not original. He's a created being. He tempts. People fall for it. He's envious and isn't plotting for your good. "You can be like God," he entices. Well, sure we can be. But only through God's saving grace, through Jesus, can we be conformed to His glory. But the devil says, "Oh, no. You don't need God. You can *be* God. Big difference, folks. And the wrong turn can be fatal. *Eternally.* So please listen up.

In addition to the biblical account, there is evidence of a massive worldwide flood, written in the earth and carried through the history of ancient people throughout the planet. Look it up. This flood was God's judgment on the ever-increasing sin of people. He did find one righteous man, Noah. With him he started over. You can read all about it in Genesis 6:9–17. Anyhoo, one of Noah's sons, Ham, turned out to be a bit of a pervert towards his own father. (Here we go again!) His dad got inadvertently slammed by strong wine and passed out. Ham inspected the nakedness of Noah and embarrassed him. After this gross disrespect, Noah cursed Ham and his descendants, who responded by increasing their rebellion against God and His ways.

Ham had a son, Cush, who wanted to build a tower that would rise so high, God wouldn't be able to bring a flood against it. Just like Eve got tempted by the devil ("You can be like God"), he set himself up as "father of the gods." Cush was the original idolater and institutor of pagan rites. His image fittingly shows him carrying a club. Also, known as Chaos (hmmm), God used him to break up the unity of people, confound their understanding, and scatter them. Ever heard of the Tower of Babel?

However, it was Cush's son, Nimrod, who actually did the building. He deified himself, claiming to be the son of god (Cush). Do you get it? The son of *god*? So Nimrod's goal was to build the tower to reach heaven. In Genesis 11:4, Moses records that God saw it, didn't like it, and confused the language so that the builders couldn't understand one another and took off in different directions. As the people scattered, they carried this false worship with them. In Egypt, Nimrod became Osiris. And in India, he became Krishna.

But wait, there's more! Nimrod had a wife, Semiramis. When Nimrod died, she deified herself, claiming to be not only his wife but his mother! Thus, she made her husband her "seed" and instituted the worship of herself as—Catholics, pay attention—"Queen of Heaven," "Madonna," "Mother of God."

You do know that Satan can read, right? Yup, he knows the Bible, and in the early part of Genesis, it says that the seed of the woman would crush the serpent's head but the serpent would wound His (the seed, a man, Jesus) heal. So old Semiramis claimed to be that woman that would bear the seed, the savior. Here's where it gets really twisted. She claimed to be her husband's mother by a virgin conception. Uh huh. Their philosophy included the transmigration of souls, or reincarnation. That's what she used to explain her getting supernaturally pregnant and giving birth to Cush after he was dead and gone. By the way, Semiramis was notoriously immoral. She did give birth to a child and ruled the people with an iron fist in his stead.

Semiramis, an actual historical person, became a "goddess," the third member of the Babylonian "trinity." She was worshipped by the names Athena, Cybil, Astoreth, Isis, Diana, and on and on. Worship included perverted sexual acts and child sacrifice. And—drum roll, please—they were known to be worshipped in the form of *rocks*! I couldn't wait to share that one with Sheila.

The dreams came like crazy that night. I woke up around 3:00 p.m. in a sweat, breathing hard. The statues I used to worship had jumped down from the altar and rushed me. Black Krishna, white

Radha, and chunky, grinning Jagannatha surrounded me. Nimai was there, too, shouting "*Traitor!*"

Trembling, I frantically searched my brain for a scripture to throw back. The Word of God, the sword of the spirit suddenly and firmly came out my mouth in the darkness, "Be not afraid of sudden fear" (Proverbs 3:25 KJV). My breathing slowed. I sat up. Obviously, reading about the historical origins of influential myths and legends had stirred this up. I knew in my intellect that they were all just toothless tigers—all growl and no bite. But in my vulnerable state of sleep, the devil, who is the real instituter of false religion, sucker punched me. I chased the night terror all the way out with "For God did not give us a spirit of fear, but of power and of love and of a sound mind" (2 Tim. 1:7 NKJ).

"God, why weren't you there in my dream to protect me?" I asked.

"I was," He whispered.

Then, I remembered hugging my dream self during this dream. But I wasn't hugging me, I was hugging Holy Spirit, Who lives in me. "You *were* there!" I cried. "Even in my sleep I took shelter of You! You drew Me to You, my ever-present help. Thank you, Holy Spirit!" I rejoiced and wrapped my arms over my chest for real and squeezed, knowing that the Spirit inside my spirit was loving me intensely.

I went back asleep. Again, I dreamed. But this one was different. In it, I picked up that silly, smiling rock from the altar, gave a good swing, and threw it at the Krishna deity. I knocked off his smug little head. It rolled to Nimai's feet. "Don't pick it up," I warned. "It's just a piece of metal. The real God loves you. His name is Jesus."

I woke up early, went for a walk all happy and perky, and then made some appetizers for Sheila and Paul's party. Later that day, when most of their guests were gone, I told Sheila about the dream. She smiled her sweet Sheila smile, hugged me, and said, "Oh, Marney, I love you so much." Yeah, I love her, too, especially when she exaggerated about how nice I looked in that size-14 dress.

Epilogue

Matthew 10:19-20 (NIV)

"But when they arrest you, do not worry about what to say or how to say it. At that time, you will be given what to say, for it will not be you speaking, but the Spirit of your Father speaking through you."

I WAS PUSHING A SHOPPING CART LADEN with my Thanksgiving groceries toward the car, when a niggling feeling had me pause. I looked to the side and spotted an elderly woman wearing a white saree. I stared. She had just gotten out of an older economy car and caught me studying her.

"Devahuti? Is that you?" she asked.

"My name is actually Marney," I replied. "But I used to be Devahuti."

"Oh, Marney, it's me, Bhakti," she said.

I pushed the cart toward her and, without hesitating, engulfed my old ashrama mother in a hug. She felt brittle as she hugged me back.

"You look great," she said, taking a small step back and assessing me.

Now, I am carrying some extra pounds, but I'm happy. Life is good. That sort of thing shows, you know? I wish I could've returned the compliment, but Bhakti looked washed out, stooped over, and trodden down. Yet, her smile and greeting were genuine, even though her voice sounded thready.

She glanced over at the cart and saw a turkey. "Oh, you eat meat," she observed.

"I'm a Christian," I explained. "I left the movement many years ago and have been saved, born again. Praise Jesus." I cocked my head and asked, "Bhakti, you're wearing a widow's saree. Did your husband pass away?"

She glanced down at her cracked, sandaled feet. "Uh, no. He took sannyasa and left to go preaching."

It occurred to me that there was no social security plan for someone like Bhakti. All these decades she'd volunteered, worked her fingers to the bone with not one dollar saved for retirement. And now, she was abandoned by her husband. Where were her children?

I asked her if I could take her out to lunch. She said the car was borrowed and she had to get back to the temple. No, her kids were living out of state, and she rarely heard from them. My heart lurched. I wanted to wrap her up and bring her home. My kids and their families were coming for the holiday, and we'd be having a great reunion, along with Sheila and Paul and their offspring.

I reached for Bhakti's boney hand, and asked if I could pray for her. She said sure. After I finished, there were tears in both our eyes. "Freedom is just a decision away," I whispered. "Jesus loves you without reservation and paid for your deliverance." I pressed my little calling card/tract with my number in her palm, along with a $20 bill.

She glanced at the card, stuck it in her bead bag, flashed a quizzical smile, and thanked me. As Bhakti walked away towards the store, I stood there, arrested. What else could I do?

After putting the groceries away, I sauntered outside and sat down in the gazebo to uncover wisdom about this encounter. A lone honeybee dipped and swooped among clover flowers. The loud tapping on one of my aging maples announced the flashy red-headed woodpecker's hunt for beetles. Honeysuckle barely tipped as an iridescent-winged hummingbird sipped nectar. Everyone was searching for sustenance.

I called Sheila.

"Well, Marney," she drawled. "You gave her an invitation to church and a scripture verse on your little card. I don't know what else you could've done under the circumstances if she was in a hurry. Holy Spirit has to draw people to Him, and they have to be receptive."

She offered to pray with me And so we did, thanking Father God in Jesus's name that many who'd been deceived by the devil, those who thought they were right with God but had actually missed the mark, would let Holy Spirit draw them to the truth of salvation through Jesus Christ.

That night as I settled in front of the fireplace with a hot mug of tea, I pleaded with the Lord once again for a mighty awakening, repentance, and revival in our nation. I prayed that the wicked become the righteous, being disgusted with the hatred and division. I begged that those who are called by His name, the Christians, kick out apostasy from the churches and embrace the full truth of the Bible without watering it down to suit worldly culture. I commanded, by the authority of Holy Spirit in me, that the fiery darts of the wicked one return to base camp, causing confusion among those who would destroy God's perfect plan. I asked God again, "What else can I do?"

"Keep praying with faith according to My Word," I heard a voice inside my insides say. "Never give up on anyone, just as I never gave up on you."

Amen.

CPSIA information can be obtained
at www.ICGtesting.com
Printed in the USA
BVHW040337221221
624596BV00016B/1571